What do Anthropologists Have to Say About Dropouts?

What do Anthropologists Have to Say About Dropouts?

The First Centennial Conference
on Children at Risk

School of Education
Stanford University

Edited by
Henry T. Trueba, George and Louise Spindler

The Falmer Press
(A member of the Taylor & Francis Group)
New York • Philadelphia • London

UK   The Falmer Press, Falmer House, Barcombe, Lewes, East Sussex, BN8 5DL

USA   The Falmer Press, Taylor & Francis Inc., 1900 Frost Road, Suite 101, Bristol, PA 19007

First published 1989

British Library Cataloguing in Publication Data

What do anthropologists have to say about dropouts?
1. United States . Schools . Dropouts . Socioculture factors
I. Trueba, Henry II. Spindler, George III. Spindler, Louise
371.2'913'0973

ISBN 1–85000–620–2
ISBN 1–85000–621–0 pbk

Jacket design by Caroline Archer

Typeset in 11/13 point Bembo by
Bramley Typesetting Limited, 12 Campbell Court, Bramley, Basingstoke, Hants.

Printed in Great Britain by
Taylor & Francis (Printers) Ltd, Basingstoke

Contents

Contents

Preface

In May 1987 a one-day seminar-conference on the relations between education and anthropology was held at the University of California, Santa Barbara (UCSB), under the auspices of the cross-cultural program and the Linguistic Minority Research Project, in the School of Education. This event was brought into being through the collaboration of Henry Trueba, Concha Delgado-Gaitan and George and Louise Spindler during the spring quarter when the Spindlers were visiting professors in the School of Education and at the Department of Anthropology at UCSB. Papers and discussions were presented by Trueba, the Spindlers, Delgado-Gaitan and Richard Duran (UCSB), Richard Warren (California Polytechnic at San Luis Obispo), Marcelo Suarez-Orozco (University of California at San Diego) and Stephen Arvizu (California State University at Bakersfield). They ranged over topics including a critique of Madeline Hunter's teaching/learning model, the life history as an approach to minority adaptations, linguistic minority family contexts and academic performance, the instrumental self and self-efficacy as factors in minority school performance and Hispanic immigrant school performance and achievement models.

These discussions were most satisfying, led in many directions and raised many issues. Our retrospective analysis at the end of the seminar-conference led us to the conclusion that there should be a follow-up conference at Stanford University the next year, focused on a current, significant educational problem about which anthropology would have something to say. We unanimously selected the dropout phenomenon that plagues our schools and to which so much recent attention has been drawn. We immediately set the wheels in motion and by the following fall had an agenda, a time, a place and the promise of financial support for a one-day conference, with a sizeable participating audience, on anthropological perspectives on dropouts. The conference was held in the conference room in the Center for Education Research at Stanford

University on 26 February 1988 as the first of a series of Stanford Centennial Conferences on children-at-risk. The format for the conference is included at the end of this Preface. This volume is the product of that conference and remains faithful to the format indicated.

We wanted the conference to be anthropologically inspired and conducted. This aim was achieved. All of the papers and responses are presented by anthropologists or people heavily influenced by anthropology and collaborating with anthropologists. Though the predominant tone is anthropological and the primary conceptual orientation is cultural, there is a healthy interdisciplinary quality to the conference. This is the way we would have it. Pure anthropology is rare, and pure anthropologists even rarer, but this volume shows us how anthropologically-inspired analyses and models, culturally oriented in concept and method, can shed light on an important, current phenomenon of great concern to educators and the general public.

The editors and conference organizers
Henry Trueba, George and Louise Spindler

A STANFORD CENTENNIAL CONFERENCE
Friday, February 26, 1988

First of a series of School of Education-Stanford Centennial Conferences
on educating children-at-risk

Schedule

8:00 a.m.   Coffee and Welcome Remarks (Larry Cuban, Associate
Dean, School of Education) Room L61 CERAS

8:15 a.m.   Focus, Expected Outcomes and Logistics
George Spindler and Henry Trueba

Introduction of Chair: Arthur P. Coladarci

Presenters	Discussants

8:30 a.m.   George and Louise Spindler   Raymond McDermott

9:15 a.m.   Henry Trueba   David Fetterman

10.00 a.m. Coffee break

10:15 a.m. Roland Tharp   Ronald Gallimore

11:00 a.m. Marcelo Suarez-Orozco   Robert Rueda

12 noon   Lunch break

1:30 p.m.   Perry Gilmore/David Smith   Concha Delgado-Gaitan

2:15 p.m.   Coffee break

2:30 p.m.   Symposium–Introduction/brief summary of proceedings to
this point
Room LGI CERAS

3:00 p.m.   Panelists' reactions and comments (Larry Cuban, chair)

4:00 p.m.   Questions, reactions from all participants and audience.
Concluding remarks.

4:30 p.m.   End of conference

JoAnn Barbour: Conference Expediter and Rapporteur
Sponsored by the School of Education, Stanford University

Grateful acknowledgment is made to the Linguistic Minority Research
Project, University of California, Santa Barbara, for contributing support.

Acknowledgments

We are grateful to the School of Education at Stanford University for financial support through the efforts of Professor Henry Levin, Dean Marshall Smith, and Development Officer Peter Treadway, and to the Linguistic Minority Research Project at the University of California, Santa Barbara, through Richard Duran. This support enabled us to invite significant contributors from places such as Alaska, Teachers College (Columbia University), Hawaii and Texas, and to provide invited participants with lodging and food as well as travel expenses, to say nothing of a delicious catered luncheon, coffee and pastries for over 100 participants.

We are especially indebted to JoAnn Barbour, who gave unselfishly of time and energy to fill the role of Expediter and Rapporteur for the Conference. We are grateful also to Elizabeth Lancefield, Olga Vasquez, Kim Lockett, and Cheryl Kettel, who acted as roving expediters during the conference, to Ruth Bergman, who handled the correspondence and many telephone calls preceding the conference, and to Gilbert Stoesz, who prepared and formatted portions of the text.

Special thanks are due to Professor Arthur Coladarci, former Dean of the School of Education at Stanford University and now Academic Secretary for the University, who acted as chair for the conference, and to Larry Cuban, then Associate Dean for Academic Affairs at the School, who acted as panel moderator.

Our deepest gratitude goes to the presenters of the papers, the discussants of papers and to the members of the participating audience. Without them there would have been no conference.

Everyone worked hard to make this conference, the first of the Centennial Conferences on Children-at-Risk for Stanford's School of Education, a success.

Henry Trueba and George and Louise Spindler have shared responsibility for all phases of conference planning and execution, from conception to realization, and to publication.

Introduction

We will make this overview brief and to the point though we are tempted to expound at length about matters that are better encountered in the conference context. We will state the major themes that we see represented and refer to some of the specific contexts where they are represented most explicitly. They are present, however, implicitly if not explicitly, in most of the papers and discussions. We will more often pose questions than generalizations or conclusions. This is the nature of the conference — that it raises questions, probes possibilities and explores contingencies but rarely arrives at conclusions, since they can be established only by careful research or by the application of ideas and theories in pragmatic action programs.

The Themes

Questioning the 'Within-Child' Deficit Model

The 'within-child' deficit model which has influenced so much of the professional thinking and action within and about our schools is challenged on every page of this report of the conference. This model ascribes school failure to deficits the child brings to school, such as IQ, and not to the total context within which a child functions. The within-child model has drawn fire from many quarters during the past decade. The anthropological perspective has played a particularly important role in this challenge. Anthropologists view the behavior of natives as a result of how natives understand their own context — in which they are trying to 'make sense'. An anthropological perspective insists that every individual does his or her best to preserve self-esteem and survive as an intact person. This struggle to preserve and survive often results in behavior that is perceived as deviant, destructive, and dysfunctional by observers who are operating out of different contexts than are those individuals being observed and evaluated — the 'natives'.

Ethnography Up-Close

Another theme that is present in some form in all of the papers and discussions, often as a basic assumption rather than as a declared statement of position, is that in order to understand matters from a native's point of view, one must study behavior in the context within which those behaviors occur. This is the basis for the challenge to the 'within-child' deficit model. Though questionnaires and neo-experimental research designs may be applied occasionally by anthropologists the customary approach is to do ethnography 'up close'. This is often referred to as 'micro-ethnography' but the distinction between micro- and macro-ethnography is not always clear. The objective of 'up close' ethnography is to come to an understanding of the native's point of view and those conditions that most directly affect the native's attempt to make sense in context. Once the school, the teacher, the classroom, the tests and sorting procedures employed in schools and the constant pressure to conform to a predetermined set of cultural standards are perceived from this point of view everything changes. The conference papers and discussions succeed in taking this position.

Macro and Micro

The macro-micro debate which has been raised in educational anthropological circles is referred to here and there within the conference format and particularly in Robert Rueda's remarks as discussant. The results of both approaches are represented. The macro level calls attention to social, political, and economic forces that affect the conditions of individual lives and school functions. The micro level approach focuses on interaction between actors in specific social contexts and upon the cultural patterns that mediate influences on individual behavior. Most anthropologists, including those represented in this conference, shift back and forth between these two approaches during the course of their research and interpretations of research results.

Success and Failure

A persistent theme throughout the conference is the observation that our educational system requires failure of some in order to assure success for others. The Spindlers, McDermott, Rueda, Trueba, Fetterman, Gilmore and Smith and the panel all make this point in some manner. The converse is that success is guaranteed by the educational system in many societies and that our own school system shows strong tendencies in this direction for the dominant middle class. This is an explicit theme in the paper by George and Louise Spindler. But as Ray McDermott points out, we spend an enormous amount of money and time locating children that we perceive as predestined for failure, often because they do not meet the expectations of the cultural patterns of the mainstream.

Are there ways we could guarantee success in our educational processing? And what would be the consequences if we did? Do we need to have approximately 25 per cent of our school population fail? Is the middle class, 'Anglo' culture the only legitimate model from which to derive expectations for success and failure? Are alternative routes possible? Is it the task of a school to transmit, preserve, and defend the Anglo-toned mainstream culture? Must one's ethnic identity be given up if that identity is in conflict with the mainstream in order to be successful in school? These questions permeate all of the papers and discussions presented in this conference. They are particularly strong in papers and discussions by the Spindlers, Suarez-Orozco, Margaret Gibson, Roland Tharp, Ronald Gallimore, Robert Rueda and Perry Gilmore and David Smith.

The Cultural Difference Hypothesis

Are cultural differences between mainstream institutions and linguistic minorities a sufficient explanation for success or failure in school? The recognition of the significance of such cultural differences is a long step away from the 'within–child' deficit model that has been held accountable so long for success or failure in school. No one argues that cultural differences are insignificant and in fact an important part of the presentations and discussions in the conference supports the significance of these differences. Education is always an *intervention* in the learning process. If the intervention is culturally incongruent with familial and community culture, conflict and miscommunication will ensue. Roland Tharp and Ronald Gallimore discuss ways in which the classroom can be made culturally compatible with the culture of the home and family of the indigenous community. The Kamahameha Early Education Program (KEEP) in Hawaii discussed by Tharp and Gallimore has demonstrated that such compatibility can be engineered and that it does ameliorate problems of adaptation, success and failure.

What Margaret Gibson, Marcello Suarez-Orozco, John Ogbu and others have demonstrated, however, is that many of the immigrants to the United States, such as the Chinese, Japanese, Korean, Vietnamese, Filipino, and Sikhs, do better in school than most of our indigenous minorities and, in some cases, better than mainstream Anglos. As Gibson points out, there is increasing evidence from the United States, Great Britain, Australia, and Canada, that children of immigrants persist in school longer and have stronger overall academic records than non-immigrant youth of similar social class backgrounds.

This is a remarkable finding and demonstrates that cultural and linguistic differences are not alone responsible for academic failure and success. Despite dramatic cultural and linguistic differences, these immigrant minorities succeed in school more frequently than do indigenous minorities with less dramatic differences in language and culture.

What are the reasons for this phenomenon? Is it merely a matter of motivation? Of compensation for feelings of guilt? Suarez-Orozco points to a combination of such factors in the academic success of Latin American refugees. They have left behind family members and friends who are subject to all of the terrors and harassment occasioned by political conflict and power struggles. Not all immigrants carry this burden of guilt and share a high degree of motivation because of it.

One factor that has not been considered sufficiently, it seems, is that the schooling these immigrants have received in their home countries may be superior in certain respects to the schooling that indigenous minorities have received in the United States, and perhaps even superior to the schooling they will receive in this country. Jose Macas argues that the schooling that Mexican immigrants received in Mexican schools tends to be more cosmopolitan and politically realistic than the schooling that children of similar age receive on this side of the border (unpublished paper). This may help account for the fact that Mexican immigrants do better in school than second- and third-generation Mexican-Americans. In any event, with attention to cross-cultural regularities in such phenomena, we are able to ask new questions about our own situation in the United States. If the children of immigrants can do relatively well in school despite deep cultural and linguistic differences and the poisonous atmosphere of the inner city, where most immigrants go, we need to understand better how they do it.

Change

One of the questions that kept reappearing during the conference was,

'How can traditional school practice be changed?' (Tharp and Gallimore, Delgado-Gaitan, Trueba, Fetterman, McDermott). There is evidence accumulating, based on ethnographic research, that changing school practice is extremely difficult. It has a tendency to persist despite dedicated efforts to reform it, and tinkering with the curriculum or with teaching techniques is useless. Attempts to change must be on a large scale and reach deep into significant relationships within the school and classroom. In the last analysis, it may be that attempts to change actual school practice are doomed to failure unless conditions change outside of the school. Society creates the need for and absorbs the product of our schools. Our concepts of success and failure and what is culturally compatible and what is not were not created by the schools. They may, however, be sustained by them. What kinds of changes and in what depth can be advocated on the basis of an anthropological perspective? This question appears here and there throughout the conference.

Dropping Out as a Sensible Solution

All of the above considerations suggest that under certain conditions and at certain times, 'dropping out' is a sensible adjustment. (Trueba, Gilmore and Smith, McDermott, and others.) When is dropping out a sensible solution? Of course, dropping out is never the most desirable solution in the long run but it may be the pragmatic one that works for the individual under conditions of stress, confrontation, conflict, and failure on the part of the school to adjust to realistic circumstances. In one way or another most of the papers and discussions at this conference dealt with this problem directly or indirectly.

Conclusion

These are the kinds of themes that appeared during the conference as we moved from paper to discussant and back to paper and finally to a panel discussion. It became clear that most of the participants were both hopeful and cynical about solutions to the dropout problem. It is also clear that the definition of the problem itself was not a matter of total agreement. Some participants even questioned that there was a dropout problem, excepting by arbitrary definition. It was also clear that most participants felt that the responsibility for the problem and for its solution did not fall wholly on the school. The school is a part of society and the conditions of school function are determined by society. Unless inequities, racism, and ethnocentrism, are reduced and the real economic and political conditions of survival and the search for happiness and security are improved for minorities the school cannot be expected to solve the problem alone. At the same time, it was recognized that the school does play an important role and that there are things that can be done in the school. The conference was shorter on solutions than on raising questions. This is appropriate, we think, to our purposes. There were, however, repeated expressions of concern about how we can translate what we *do know* into practice. How can basic research be translated into practice? asked Tharp, Gallimore, Delgado–Gatain, Fetterman, McDermott, and participants in the panel discussion.

We hope that readers will get some ideas about how we may apply what we do know by reading and thinking about the content of this conference, *What Do Anthropologists Have to Say About Dropouts?* To arrive at a sober evaluation of such application, however, has not been the major purpose of the conference. Our purpose has been to raise significant questions and give those questions sufficient context to make them intelligible. We think that the conference succeeded in doing that.

Chapter 1

There Are No Dropouts among the Arunta and Hutterites

George and Louise Spindler
Department of Anthropology and School of Education,
Stanford University.

We intend this paper to be cross-cultural, holistic and anthropological in the traditional sense of the discipline. Much current work in school ethnography has been micro-analytic rather than holistic and it has been confined to our own schools without comparative reference. Attention to the inner dynamics of the classroom, and even to smaller segments such as reading groups, has been productive. The broader comparative scope, however, can give us useful perspective on our schools and our assumptions about education. To do this we will regard schooling as a form of cultural transmission, and we will be particularly concerned with a special form of cultural transmission called 'initiation'. In the course of our analysis we will make various broad statements about education that express our understanding of the phenomenon. Though they may seem assertive, they are to be taken as tentative and subject to modification or replacement as our understanding grows.

Assumptions

All human societies purposefully educate their young. All humans, as advanced primates, are superlearners. They will learn anything and everything if not interfered with. Children in all societies, however, learn only certain things. All educational systems are intentional interferences with the learning process — so children learn what adults think they should learn, and do not learn what adults think they should not — presumably. Of course, what adults think they are teaching their children and what children actually learn may be rather different. The success of an educational system in the restricted sense of the term may be measured by the discrepancy.

In our cross-cultural studies we have called attention to a process we have termed 'cultural compression'. Humans spend a lot of time and energy compressing their offspring into the cultural mold. They do so because education, as cultural transmission, is the major mechanism of cultural survival. Cultural survival requires replication to the extent possible. Education, seen from this point of view, functions to recruit new members into society and maintain the cultural system (G. Spindler, 1970, 1974; G. and L. Spindler, 1982).

One of the major cultural compression, recruitment and maintenance processes worldwide is what anthropologists have called 'rites of passage' or initiation ceremonies (Van Gennep, 1960; Young, 1965). These may be seen as high points in cultural transmission and acquisition, where the moral force and social energies of the community are brought to bear on the initiate, to shape him or her into the desired and valued adult mold. They constitute the most explicit forms of intentional cultural transmission — the most formal expression of education — in most of the world's culture.

These periods of initiation, of compressive cultural transmission, vary greatly in intensity and duration from society to society. In some cases, as among the Fore of the Highlands of New Guinea, there is scarcely a notice of the transition of girls and boys into adulthood though much is made of funerals (Sorenson, 1967). As among others, such as the central desert people of aboriginal Australia (Spencer and Gillen, 1899, 1904), the Sambia of the New Guinea Islands (Herdt, 1981, 1987) or the Sebei of Africa (Goldschmidt, 1976, 1987), the initiations start early in life and continue in a highly compressive sequence of intensive periods of activity, in some cases lasting for a decade or more.

One of the primary mechanisms that make the initiation process effective as an educational device appears to be the resolution of dissonance, in the original sense of the term proposed by Leon Festinger (1957). That is, the experience of sudden compressive initiation, discontinuous with the previous experience of the child, creates anxiety and produces ambivalence toward the very cultural system and its representatives that are managing the initiation. This anxiety and ambivalence, which can be termed dissonance for our purposes, is resolved by the successful completion of the initiation sequence, and virtually all initiates do complete the process. The initiation proceedings are not designed to produce failure. They produce success. As this dissonance is resolved, the initiates identify with and internalize the attributes of the personnel, the values and symbols deemed important by the adult preceptors running the show. We may be able to convey the essential nature of this model of education by describing some of the sequences of initiations for the traditional Arunta of central desert Australia. We will use the ethnographic present in our description (Spencer and Gillen, 1899, 1904).

There are seven stages of initiation for Arunta males. We will not discuss the females; they are no less important than the males, but their initiation is focused mostly on one point in the life cycle — marriage. The males start their formal education at about age 10 and it continues into the 20s in most cases. The initiation begins with the Ambaquerka stage, when the boys are seized and taken from the bosom of their families by forbidding strangers. They are transported away into the night to an isolated camp in the bush. This separation from family and home is a persistent feature of initiations everywhere. While in the bush camp, the initiates are treated to considerable physical hazing, including being tossed in the air, smoked over fires and having some front teeth knocked out. While all this is happening, their preceptors are teaching them how important it is to keep secret all they learn, and giving them some glimpses into the structure of meaning surrounding creation and life. After a week the boys are returned to their home camp much chastened and enjoined not to talk about what has happened and to avoid all direct contact with their mothers and sisters. Secrecy and cross-sex avoidance are also near universals.

Within a year or two the young initiates will enter the next stage of initiation when a large gathering called a Corroboree is held. This stage of initiation, which includes a number of substages, culminates in circumcision, done with great ceremony, and as a kind of reinforcement of deep lessons learned and never to be forgotten concerning the time of origin — the dream time — and the Churingas — sacred objects connecting humans to the dream time. They also learn the obligations of kinship, as roles of instruction, support and hazing are distributed among kin. Among the Arunta kinship is very complex. During all the ceremonies the initiates huddle together, underfed, cold, scared, and denied anything resembling human status or participation in the normal round of Arunta culture. Nor are they permitted any casual social participation in their own peer group. Life is earnest, their preceptors severe and their future in seeming doubt.

To make matters worse, there is a constant battle being fought between the males at one end of the ceremonial grounds, where the initiates are literally held captive, and the females, including mothers and sisters, at the other end. The women surge forth, armed with shields and clubs, beat the men savagely and return triumphant to their end of the arena with the initiates they have recaptured. But soon the men invade the women's area, seize the initiates and return to their end. This happens several times. The boys are the object of a greal deal of attention and conflict, all of it threatening.

During the days and nights of the initiation, for this particular stage, the boys are taught more and more about the dream time, the Churingas (sacred icons), and the network of kin obligations. They are also learning respect, obedience and gender roles. The physical hazing continues and one day, as the high point of the Ulpmerka stage, the initiates are seized, one by one, laid across a living table constituted of the backs of kneeling men, and circumcised with a chipped stone blade. They are not allowed a whimper or a cry. When finished, they have passed into the Arakatura stage and are semi-adult.

But the initiate still does not have full access to his Churingas or their totemic and sacred storage place, or to the innermost secrets of Arunta theology and cosmology. This will come later as he nears complete manhood and is admitted to the inner circle of power and knowledge. Another large Corroboree is held. Many rituals are held by the various totems and lineages assembled, but the most important is the staging of the final initiations for the 'graduating class'.

Again the males and females are segregated for ritual purposes during the days and nights of the ceremony. The symbolic battle for possession of the initiates goes on, the instruction in the esoteric and sacred aspects of Arunta culture continues under the most dramatic conditions imaginable. The climax is the subincision, when each initiate is again seized, laid down and held down on the living table of human backs, and his penis cut to the urethra its entire length. When this final event occurs the women wail, tear their hair and rub ashes on open wounds. The young men rouse from their state of shock and each grasps a boomerang furnished for that purpose, hurls it towards the female encampment, and sings a song directed at his mother which says, 'And now I am through with that place.' The boy has become a man and now has access to all of the secrets and power his culture affords. His dissonance is resolved. He is now Urliara — finished. He is committed forever to his culture, its values, beliefs and ideology and to male authority. Despite the onerous nature of the initiation, instruction and experience, and the dissonance aroused, all of the young initiates survive the ordeal and are dedicated to seeing that the next class of initiates gets the same treatment.

All of the initiates succeed, none fail, in this intensive, compressive school. To fail would mean at least that one could not be an Arunta, and usually this must mean death as well, but not death at the hands of another, but social death, which in most societies means physical death. The whole operation of the initiation school is managed to produce success. To fail to initiate the young males successfully is unthinkable. The continuity of culture would be broken and the society would disintegrate. There are no dropouts.

The Arunta are an exotic, traditional, non-Western technologically primitive people. It will be instructive to look at some similar processes among a Western culture group — the Hutterites (Hostetler and Huntington, 1980). They number some 20,000 people today, but only 300 when they fled to North America from Europe, persecuted for generations because of their anti-infant baptism beliefs. They live in communal colonies in the prairies of the western United States and Canada. They regard education as the most important instrument of survival, and they commit themselves unstintingly to its proper execution. Formal education among the Hutterites is functionally equivalent to the prolonged initiation in its multiple stages for the Arunta. The process starts with kindergarten at age 3, after a fairly unpressured early childhood. In kindergarten children do not play with toys or model clay. They sit at a table on long benches and learn to pray, sing hymns and repeat religious phrases. They may play at times with something like burnt matches in a box or a clothespin that they have brought with them. They do have naps and snacks, but by any mainstream standard the Hutterite kindergarten is a spare, compressive environment.

At age 6 they enter two schools — one the state or provincial mandated elementary school, the other their own German school — held before and after hours for the first school, and on Saturday. German school is run by a man who often walks about with a switch or strap and uses it when necessary. He never punishes in anger, only in sorrow, and to make good Hutterites. There is nothing personal about it.

At age 16 the children leave school and join the work force, travelling from colony to colony as a group. These are the 'foolish years' when courtship occurs and a certain amount of tomfoolery is tolerated, if not sanctioned. Girls paint their toes with fingernail polish, worn inside their heavy shoes, and boys affect a jaunty, if somewhat somber, cowboy style. These foolish years pass quickly and usually by the early 20s, though there are some holdouts, both sexes are asking for baptism, religious instruction and then marriage. After this the long road of Hutterite conformity follows until death.

Again, despite the massive interference, the heavy compression of Hutterite schooling, the system produces only success. There are no failures, and no dropouts. There is resistance, anxiety and dissonance along the way. As one young male Hutterite, whose name also happened to be George, said to me, 'George, you couldn't stand to be a Hutterite for three seconds!' Some of the young men delay baptism and marriage into the late 20s and even into the 30s but all finally succumb.

But the doubts are resolved by the process of education. Hutterite education is one long initiation process, as are all educational systems seen from the point of view we are presenting. The initiate is committed to the cultural system by experiencing its managed, intentional, compressive, educational interference with learning, and experiencing it successfully. The reward is becoming what one's preceptors want one to be — a Hutterite.

We will add only one other culture to our list of examples — our own, as we experienced it. We are both 100 per cent mainstream ethnic WASPS. We both went to school in places where there was ethnic and social class diversity. We both came from middle-class homes. My father was a professor in the local teachers' college. Louise's father was a self-made lawyer, a real estate developer and a politician. Our mothers were both homemakers but also active in social and community life. We both found the initiation ceremonies of our culture tedious at times. Our American initiation, our culturally constructed intentional interference in learning, begins early and lasts long. Much of it seems irrelevant — at least it did to us. The school was confining, it took up most of the day, it interfered with much else we wanted to do.

But our success, like that of the Arunta and Hutterite children, was assumed and assured. We had special classes with special teachers. We skipped grades and participated in progressive educational experiments. When we performed poorly, our teachers made an effort to find out what was wrong and how it could be corrected. I went through high school with a cohort group of some thirty-five similar young people. We had all the best teachers and all the most interesting opportunities, much less available to the numerically dominant Polish Catholic majority of second generation immigrants. I (George) still found school oppressive and interfering, and I learned the more important lessons of carpentry, logic, esthetics and Latin from my father and not in the school. Louise minded it less, as girls usually do, though she claims her more positive attitude was due to the fact that she went to school in southern California, which was Lotusland in her day.

All of my cohort group in my small mid-western community went on to college. Nearly all became professionals and have had successful American mainstream lives and careers. No one that I knew even considered dropping out of school, and all were confident that there would be a place in society for them at the end of the long initiation ritual we call schooling. Louise's experience was broadly similar.

Interpretive Conclusion

The main point to our comparative analysis is a simple one and one that most of us recognize, and that is that school, just as in the Arunta and Hutterite cases, and in thousands of other cultures, is borne, endured, survived, accomplished, because it is geared to success, not failure, and because success mean a place, a productive, acceptable place in the social, economic and honorific scheme of things. There is an assured and assumed continuity, whatever the compressions, constraints, threats and anxiety aroused may be. The system is self-sustaining. The outcome assures the reduction of dissonance and identification with desired goals; and the cultural system has recruited new members committed to its maintenance.

These are precisely the conditions that many minorities do not encounter and the experience they do not have (Jacobs and Jordan, 1987). The school experience early on defines them as potential failures or even learning disabled, and there is always the implication that even if they put up with such definitions and endure the school, they are not assured of a positive gain at the end. The long initiation ritual of the school is for many minorities a long drawn out degradation ritual. Their language is criticized, their style disparaged and their origins suspect. Often these intimations are very subtle, and corrections of behaviors and style are offered by teachers and sometimes by peers with the most worthy of explicit intentions.

Further, according to some analysts, certain indigenous minorities have developed a culture of resistance to schooling administered in its mainstream form (Erickson, 1987). This culture of resistance is formed out of the long experience of these minorities in an essentially racist society. As with all cultures, it may continue to persist when it is not an effective adaptation to reality. This cultural resistance casts the school and teachers as enemies, with whom cooperation is suspect and to whom submission is disloyalty to one's own peer group or even to one's home and family. It is as though some of the initiates in our schools had decided that they were being initiated into the wrong society, into the enemy camp.

Schooling in America is not experienced in the same way by all minorities, as everyone knows by now. Blacks, Mexican Americans and native Americans are more frequently alienated by schooling than are Asiatics and many of the new immigrants such as the Punjabis. In fact, the latter two populations seem frequently to find the school experience a major instrumental path to success (Gibson, 1987). Nor is schooling in America experienced in the same way by Blacks, Mexican Americans or native Americans. Increasing numbers of all minorities are achieving success in school and success, as measured by mainstream standards, in United States society, even at the same time as the proportion of dropouts is increasing in some areas.

The initiation rituals of the school in America must be endured, just as the initiations for the Arunta and Hutterites must be endured, if our children are to become functioning adults in our society. The initiation rituals of the Arunta and Hutterites are designed for, in fact guaranteed, success. Our initiation rituals seem designed to assure success for some, and failure for others (Goldman and McDermott, 1987).

Our analytic model suggests that success is what we need to study. The reasons for dropping out seem more apparent than the reasons for staying in. We need to examine the factors involved in the relative success of some groups, but we also need to examine more critically the factors involved in the school success of individuals. Nor should mainstream schools or mainstream children be neglected. There are many degrees of alienation expressed among mainstream children in even 'good' schools. What keeps mainstream children in school even under conditions of fairly heavy alienation? We might find that our prolonged initiation rituals, our intentional interferences with learning, have become less functionally related to life in our society and our time than we think. If the school can be made a pathway to success for everyone, there will be no dropouts.

References

ERICKSON, FREDERICK (1987) 'Transformation and school success: The politics and culture of educational achievement', *Anthropology and Education Quarterly*, **18**, 4: pp. 313–34.

FESTINGER, LEON (1957) *A Theory of Cognitive Dissonance*, Stanford, CA: Stanford University Press.

GIBSON, MARGARET (1987) 'Punjabi immigrants in an American high school', in G. and L. SPINDLER (Eds.) (1987) *Interpretive Ethnography of Education*, Hillsdale, NJ: Lawrence Erlbaum Associates.

GOLDMAN, SHELLEY, V. and MCDERMOTT, RAY (1987) 'The culture of competition in American schools', in G. SPINDLER (Ed.), *Education and Cultural Process: Anthropological Approaches*, 2nd ed. Prospect Heights, IL: Waveland Press.

GOLDSCHMIDT, WALTER (1976) *The Culture and Behavior of the Sebei: A Study in Continuity and Adaptation*, (with the assistance of Gale Goldschmidt) Berkeley, CA: University of California Press.

GOLDSCHMIDT, WALTER, (1987) 'The Sebei: A Study in Adaptation, in G. and L. SPINDLER, (Eds.), *Case Studies in Cultural Anthropology*, New York: Holt, Rinehart and Winston.

HERDT, GILBERT, H. (1981) *Guardians of the Flutes: Idioms of Masculinity*, New York: McGraw-Hill.

HERDT, GILBERT, H. (1987) 'The Sambia: Ritual and gender in New Guinea', in G. and L. SPINDLER (Eds.), *Case Studies in Cultural Anthropology*, New York: Holt, Rinehart and Winston.

HOSTETLER, JOHN and HUNTINGTON, G. (1980) 'The Hutterites in North America', in G. and L. SPINDLER (Eds.), *Case Studies in Cultural Anthropology*, New York: Holt, Rinehart and Winston.

JACOB, E. and JORDAN, C. (Guest Editors) (1987) *Explaining the school performance of minority students*, Theme issue of the *Anthropology of Education Quarterly*, **18**, 4: pp. 259–392.

JACOBS, EVELYN and JORDAN, CATHIE (Eds.) (1987) 'Theme Issue: Explaining the school performance of minority students', *Anthropology and Education Quarterly*, **18**, 4.

SORENSON, RICHARD (1967) 'Fore Childhood.' Unpublished doctoral dissertation, Stanford University.

SPENCER, BALDWIN and GILLEN, F. J. (1899) *The Native Tribes of Central Australia*. Republished in 1965 by Dover Press, New York.

SPENCER, SIR BALDWIN and GILLEN, F. J. (1904) *The Northern Tribes of Central Australia*. Republished in 1965 by Dover Press, New York.

SPINDLER, GEORGE (1970) 'The education of adolescents: An anthropological perspective', in ELLIS D. EVANS (Ed.), *Readings in Behaviorial Development*, Hinsdale, IL: Dryden Press.

SPINDLER, GEORGE (1974) 'Cultural transmission', in G. SPINDLER (Ed.), *Education and Cultural Process*, New York: Holt, Rinehart and Winston. Reprinted in G. and L. SPINDLER (1987) *Education and Cultural Process: Anthropological Approaches*, 2nd ed., Prospect Heights, IL: Waveland Press.

SPINDLER, GEORGE and SPINDLER, LOUISE (1982) 'Do anthropologists need learning theory?' *Anthropology and Education Quarterly*, **13**, 2: pp. 109–25. Reprinted in G. SPINDLER (Ed.), *Education and Cultural Process: Anthropological Approaches*, 2nd ed., Prospect Heights, IL: Waveland Press.

VAN GENNEP, ARNOLD (1960) *Rites of Passage*. Chicago, IL: University of Chicago Press.

YOUNG, FRANK W. (1965) *Initiation Ceremonies: A Cross-Cultural Study of Status Dramatization*, Indianapolis, IND: Bobbs-Merrill.

Discussant's Comments: Making Dropouts

Raymond P. McDermott
Teachers College, Columbia University

To any generalization about the human situation anthropologists are usually ready to counter with a description of a people — usually by the name of /mai pipl/ — who are an exception to the rule. For this reason Wallace (1968) has called anthropology the 'science of the anecdotal veto'. This venerable tradition was put at the heart of American anthropology by Franz Boas (1928) and the founders of the *Journal of Applied Anthropology* (1941), but as a culture we have proceeded pretty much without a knowledge that most of our social problems are either handled differently or do not even exist in other cultures. Although we have not made enough use of it, people working on education have had the anthropological tradition available for over thirty years due to the pioneering work of George Spindler (1955, 1959) and Jules Henry (1963, 1972). In 'There Are No Dropouts among the Arunta and Hutterites' George and Louise Spindler (1988) offer their latest use of an anthropological veto to stimulate new and critical ways to think about a currently pressing social issue. My comments offer both an appreciation of their effort and some ideas on how to make us of it.[1]

The anthropological maxim is clear: kids in every culture on record learn what has to be learned and do what has to be done to live in their culture. How then could we have so many of our young unable or unwilling to finish high school, unless we are in fact, in ways unknown to our hard working parents and teachers, organizing high school as a place from which it makes sense to drop out? By dropping out or staying in, either way, our children are performing two of the essential roles made available to them by American culture. That the one (dropping out and school failure) is consciously frowned on by adults does not mean that it is not essential to the maintenance of its alternative (staying in school

16

and academic success); a high dropout rate means that, culturally speaking, many are being invited to drop out. We may have dug ourselves into a hole, from which the anthropologist, who sees all cultures as collections of people well organized to dig themselves further into their own problems, may offer a moment of relief.

In showing how the dropout problem could be otherwise, the Spindler paper forces us to consider a few ways to understand the veto power of anthropological anecdotes. For the past twenty years I have been presenting educators with accounts of the learning achievements of children in societies without schools. If the Vaupes Indians of Colombia can learn ten languages in the course of growing up (Jackson, 1974), how could we have a nation of children who cannot master French, Spanish, or even a slightly different dialect of English? If the Hanunoo from the mountain tops of Mindoro (Philippines) can achieve a high rate of literacy without any formal instruction and in a script that does not fit the spoken language of the people (Conklin, 1949), how could we have a literacy problem in American schools with ten years of compulsory attendance? If the seafarers of medieval Europe could learn to handle the shifting tides of their northern seas and the shifting times of their nascent calendars and clocks without elaborate navigational instruments (Frake, 1984), how could we have a numeracy problem after our children spend years doing arithmetic?

These can be interesting questions in some circumstances, but they do not offer comfort to the people caught in the middle of American school struggles. There is some comfort in knowing that everyone can learn difficult things if their culture organizes it for them, but the people in our schools think they must know, by Monday morning, how to organize more learning for their children in school. There is some comfort to the parents of a child labeled LD that there are countries, Denmark and Japan, for example, where there are both high success rates and few children formally labeled as broken (Downing, 1973). But there is not much comfort: the parents need more than an idea that things could possibly be different; they need some things to do, they need to help and they need some control over the lives of their children. Short of asking the parents to move to Denmark or Japan, of what use is the anthropological instinct? Can the anecdotal veto help us to reorganize?

Although we seem stuck between the homeless wisdom of anthropology and the immediate needs of our children, our situation may be much more workable than first appears. We must look more carefully at the anthropological position. The point is not just that people elsewhere have different problems. The more important point is that problems are culturally constructed. People in different cultures drive each other crazy in different ways; whatever the methods employed, they will be finely tuned to all aspects of life in the particular culture under analysis. School failure is not the horror everywhere that it is here: among the Mehinaku shortness will suffice (Gregor, 1977); among the Chagga it is marriage failure that will attract the most negative attention (Moore, 1976); among the Apache nothing could be worse than being a show-off with all the answers (Basso, 1979). School defined intelligence is only one dimension along which people can be graded and degraded, and a rather unimportant one in many cultures (Dexter, 1964; Edgerton, 1970). Even in the society that perhaps put the heaviest demands on the cognitive and literacy skills of its young, namely Imperial China, a sloppy handwriting or even a raindrop on a paper submitted on the district examinations could have a person punished for having a moral flaw, no matter how good the content (Miyazaki, 1981). From a long list of foolish alternatives for ranking people, we can cite: fat/thin, strong/weak, black/white, rich/poor, fertile/barren, articulate/inarticulate and so on. From a more interesting list of alternatives, we might focus on societies in which the grading and degrading is not the only game in town, societies in which people are more accepted for what they can do and not crushed for what they cannot do (Selby, 1976). Cultures can cut the deck in many ways. We only know for sure that every deck will be loaded; every culture will make demands without supplying most of what its members need to meet those demands; for example, the Chinese district examinations were taken in tiny three-sided huts that offered little protection from the rain.

If cultures construct their own problems, where might the people in a culture find solutions? Clearly, to do so, they have to change their culture. In American culture it has become shockingly clear that we do not send our children to school to learn to read and write, but to read and write better than their neighbors. We know this from looking closely at how our children measure themselves against each other at appointed times in every classroom in the country. We know this from looking at parents reading their children's report cards and figuring out where they stand relative to each other. We know this from looking at the success of the testing industry. The only solution to anyone's educational problem in America is to have that person do better than someone else, preferably better than half of the someone else's, and for a maximum of mobility better than all of the someone elses. School success comes hard in America. The very tools we have for making some people successful drive other people down. When anthropologists notice that school failure is a culturally constructed problem, they notice as well that culturally it is a problem we are not well tooled to solve (Goldman and McDermott, 1987).

If anthropologists do nothing more than point out the irony of our situation, they should be among the blessed for being intellectually stimulating and for encouraging us to laugh at ourselves.[2] To have serious, rigorous and respectful clowns working for the culture and pointing to our foibles and self-created disabilities is the hallmark of a culture worth living in (Bakhtin, 1940/1984; Boon, 1984). But there is something more in the anthropological critique of America. There is the invitation to change the culture, the invitation to forge new tools for helping our children by organizing new and more intelligent problems around which they might fail. Suppose the goal were not to be better than some proportion of everyone else; suppose the goal were simply to be good at something, be it baseball, anthropology or helping someone else to get through life. As a youngster, I was told that the goal of life was to be good at something and to help others. What might we have to change to make this possible for our children? How much of our culture might we have to change to restructure the mindless competition around arbitrary ends, the consequences of which are defined more by available slots in the right college or the job market than by any student's excellence? What might we have to do to return competition to its rightful place as a great way to motivate orderly practice among equals, rather than a fight to institutional death among individuals very differently prepared for performance on arbitrary school tasks and test items?

Let us focus more directly on the problem of high school dropouts. The claim by Spindler and Spindler is clear: there are whole cultures in faraway lands and even subcultures nearer our midst without such a problem. The Arunta and the Hutterites are a good way to state the case. People in those places grow by following their nose, much like the rest of us. There is a difference, however. Their collective nose leads to participation, and participation leads them eventually to a formal moment of inclusion in the membership. Our collective nose leads to participation, and it is by virtue of our participation that half of us do well and half of us fail — half above grade level and half below — at every stage in school. Eventually even participation — the kind that school officials count anyway — drops off. So do the kids, and we have a problem.

That we have a problem with dropouts does not tell us what our problem is or what we should do about it. The anthropological intervention begins with the basic suspicion that a problem named is a more important problem hidden. Fifty years ago most of our children did not finish high school, but we did not have a named dropout problem. Why do we count now and not then? What gets counted anyway? A recent government publication gives us the following definition of a dropout (Office of Educational Research and Improvement, 1987): 'A pupil who leaves school, for any reason except death, before graduation or completion of a program of studies and without transferring to another school.' What are we getting from gathering data with such a wide ranging definition? Mindless precision, perhaps; the government reports that 3789 children join the ranks every day.[3] But what is the dropout problem? What might be a solution? And why should we start our inquiry with the Arunta and the Hutterites?

Examples from the Arunta and the Hutterites, and we might just as well include the enviable, single digit dropout rate among the highly competitive Japanese (Rohlen, 1983), force us to consider the possibility that our children who drop out of school are in fact being perfectly normal members of our culture. Our schools divide people into halves: those who can and those who cannot. Dropouts are doing what the culture tells those in the losing half to do: they are getting out of the way. There are thousands of students every day who are insured success simply because the dropouts have disappeared from the competitive roles. Where would the successful be without dropouts? From the first grade on, the instructions seem clear: dropping out is one way to go.

Students drop out for a wide range of reasons, enough of them relating to economic difficulties to make social class and minority group membership key variables in their description (Fine, 1986; Mann, 1986). The personal reasons for dropping out are complex enough to overwhelm the vocabulary we have for describing the outcomes. Institutionally we stick to a simple language: either they are in school or they are out; if they are out, they are a problem that we should worry about and try to fix; if we are going to fix the problem, we need to know who the problem children are and we must change them with programs that reshape their values, alter their perceptions and put them on the right road. That is the logic of our common sense.

The anthropologist here counters with an alternative. Suppose part of the problem is our common sense, the shovel with which we dig ourselves further into our hole. Perhaps the issue is neither the individuals nor their choices. Indeed, whatever their choices, whether they drop out in order to help at home, raise their own children or sell drugs, or even if they drop out to protest the inadequacies of the system or to respond to a locally realistic assessment that a high school degree will not help them much, we classify them simply as dropouts. There may be a more telling way to view them, and it is well stated by Michelle Fine (1986: 407):

> . . . perhaps most compelling is to consider what would happen, in our present-day economy, to these young men and women

if they all graduated. Would their employment and/or poverty prospects improve individually as well as collectively? Would the class, race, and gender differentials be eliminated or even reduced? Or does the absence of a high school diploma only obscure what would otherwise be obvious conditions of structural unemployment, underemployment, and marginal employment disproportionately endured by minorities, women, and low-income individuals.

In such an economy it makes sense that we have schools in which everyone must do better than everyone else. It does not have to be that way, of course. Education could be geared to excellence without the systematic destruction of those who are less excellent or, at the start of school, totally unprepared for excellence. Unfortunately, in America, we have given up a concern for excellence in exchange for a rhetoric of excellence that lives off the propensity of some who are better prepared than others to do better than others on arbitrary tasks in school. However complex the decisions of our young men and women to drop out, however large their potential for learning in the long run, we have only the success and failure piles to sort them into, and these piles seem well organized by some brutal facts about opportunity in our economy. This is no easy connection to change. 'Arbitrary' cultural categories and 'real' economic facts are a powerful combination.

The anthropological argument can point to some ways to initiate change. The category of dropout is arbitrary in the sense that it could be otherwise, as among the Arunta and Hutterites who have no use of it. To make an arbitrary category look real requires great work on the parts of many people constraining each other into institutional pathways that lead to simplified, overdetermined outcomes, for example, good/bad student, smart/dumb, employable/unemployable. In the case of dropouts we have a school system preoccupied with the location, documentation, explanation and remediation of apparent failure, and that system has been directed of late to the creation, measurement and remediation of dropouts. Enough people are paying attention to dropouts that the category has become real, enough for 3789 persons to join as members everyday. The anthropologist can counter that the dropout problem is arbitrary in the sense that it could be otherwise, but this does not erase the fact that a tremendous amount of institutional energy is directed to dropout recognition. Worse, it is clear that all this energy is well fitted to some harsh economic realities. The Spindler veto of the dropout problem has led us in the right direction. Yes, if the Arunta and the Hutterites can live without it, as we did until not long ago, so we can live without it once again. But it will not happen by fiat. The anthropological veto carries no legislative power.

Anthropologists interested in change must focus on all the work that goes into the recognition of dropouts and organize to mobilize and redirect that work to other ends. The category dropout may be arbitrary, but it is oppressively real to those so categorized. Fine (1986) has noted that many who are called dropouts are in fact put out of school. Like many labels pointing to educational deficits, the dropout category has become carnivorous: it eats thousands of young people daily. The category LD is ready to acquire our youngest school problems; the category dropout is ready to acquire our young adults; and the category unemployable or illiterate is ready to acquire our adults (McDermott, 1988; Smith, 1986). What are we to do if our culture is producing categories that are leading to our own destruction? What are we to do when, to paraphrase Jules Henry (1963), culture works against its own people?

The anthropological critique suggests three roads to change. The first is shared with the rest of American culture: fix the kids who are broken, help them to stay in school and to become productive workers. Try anything that works. Don't stop trying and celebrate every local level success. At the same time, and this is where the anthropology differs from other social policy efforts, expect the problem to get worse. To the extent that the nation is mobilized to identify and remediate any group of unfortunates, to the extent that their problems become the focus of budget lines and institutions that rely on the problems to define themselves, that is the extent to which things will get worse. Imagine the bite on educational budgets if everyone were to stay in school and do well.[4] In a community divided as ours by class and racial borders, schools cannot be expected to exist as if in a vacuum put aside for cognitive growth. If a struggle between the haves and have-nots dominates the wider community, the same struggle will be played out in every classroom and every category applied to every child. As soon as a new problem is named, it can be used equally by people trying to solve the problem and people prospering from the existence of the problem; the complexity of the situation can be grasped in the realization that it is often the same people who help and prosper at the same time. In times of economic growth this struggle may be resolved on the side of the helpers; when there are fewer resources to go around, those who prosper carry the day.

A second road to change would have us confronting the institutional forces that are so well organized to document disabilities and negative traits among our school children. We can worry about the children later; first, we must confront the narrow world of opportunity that they are offered; we must confront the simplified, overdetermined and statistically mandated categories into which they can be graded and degraded. Here the anthropological veto can play a major role. If most of the world's cultures can do without failure and high rates of alienation and dropping out, why can't we? Failure is our problem, not failing children. Who can we trust to work for the success of all children, who still stand up to the testing industry or to parents who want their children to do better than everyone else? How can we make life easier for such persons? In addition to more educational opportunities, dropouts need a class action suit on their behalf against the industry of definitions and remediation programs that will likely do them more harm than good.

A third road to change is least direct and most important. The dropout problem is a political problem and should be handled as such. It is a problem around which we can organize protest and reform. That the category of dropout is primarily a category of blame points to the problem and identifies both the victims and the culprits, those who are labeled and those who do the blaming. If the culture and political economy of the country were different, we might not have a dropout problem. We might not need dropouts. If there were adequate jobs waiting for all, there would not be a dropout problem; perhaps companies would raid high schools, and we could have a 'pulled-out' problem on our hands. Similarly, if we did not have an abundance of psychological tests for finding our children, from their first days in school, lacking in various ways, we would not have so many poised to leave high school before finishing. We have a system that is well designed to make dropouts. This is a political problem and will not give way until we struggle to disconnect schooling from the distribution of resources throughout the country. Few cultures can afford to let their members know what their problems are; the rest prefer to keep everyone busy chasing shadows. The dropout problem is such a shadow until we use it to confront the more pressing problem, namely, the increasing divide between those who have and those who do not.

The anthropological veto has the great advantage of not letting us believe that our most obvious problems are easily available to us for analysis and solution. To that we can add the political point, namely, that the ways in which we misperceive our problems are well organized aspects of the system that keeps us in our respective places in a hierarchy of access to goods. Work on any social problem must make the fight against inequality its first priority. If we really want to know what the dropout problem is, we must challenge those who use the term and locate their allegiances. Every occasion for the use of the term 'dropout' can be examined for its attachments to the wider political arena. Enough experience of this kind might net us the power to use the term 'dropout' as a rallying cry for those who have been left out against those who run our credentialing institutions. The road from anthropological veto to political action should be short.

Notes

1 These comments focus on the work of the Spindlers on the anthropology of education. This should not obscure their parallel contribution to the anthropology of America. For the latter see their review (Spindler and Spindler, 1983).
2 For an unusually wry account of the anthropological enterprise, there are the words of Samuel Beckett's Molloy (1955:37): 'What I liked about anthropology was its inexhaustible faculty of negation, its relentless definition of man, as though he were no better than God, in terms of what he is not.'
3 The Office of Education definition offers no guidance on how to count suicide, the ultimate dropout strategy. More serious accounts of the inadequacy of the dropout data by various definitions can be found in Hammock (1986) and Morrow (1986).
4 It is easy to argue that dropouts are an economic burden, so easy in fact that the anthropologist insists on going the opposite direction and asking about who might be profiting from such an overall bad deal. Mann (1986) argues that, given the low salaries afforded to dropouts across their working career, we will lose 71 billion dollars in social security if we continue at a 25 per cent dropout rate. Arbitrary categories from education seem to go deep in our economic thinking as well. Mann also argues that Japanese dominance in various manufacturing fields stems from the lack of education among our dropouts. Given the cultural complexity of Japanese economic success, this is a foolish argument. Imagine how the lives of American dropouts or manufacturers would have to be altered for us to model the Japanese work force. The anthropological veto can be used to counter accepted practices in economic reasoning (Bilmes, 1985).

References

BAKHTIN, MIKHAIL (1940/1984) *Rabelais and His World*, Bloomington, IND: Indiana University Press.
BECKETT, SAMUEL (1955–58) *Malloy, Malone Dies, The Unnamable*, New York: Grove Press.
BILMES, JACK (1985) 'Freedom and Regulation: An anthropological critique of free market ideology', *Research in Law and Economics*, **7**: pp. 123–47.
BOAS, FRANZ (1928) *Anthropology and Modern Life*, New York: W. W. Norton.
BOON, JAMES (1984) 'Folly, Bali, and anthropology, or satire across cultures', in EDWARD BRUNER (Ed.), *Text, Play, and Story*, pp. 156–77. Washington: American Ethnological Society.

CONKLIN, HAROLD (1949) 'Hanunoo literacy', *Pacific Discovery*, **3**: pp. 4–11.

DEXTER, LEWIS (1964) 'On the politics and sociology of stupidity in our society', in H. BECKER (Ed.), *The Other Side*, pp. 37–50. New York: Free Press.

DOWNING, JOHN (1973) *Comparative Reading*, New York: Macmillan.

EDGERTON, ROBERT (1970) 'Mental retardation in non-Western societies: Toward a cross-cultural perspective in incompetence', in H. C. HAYWOOD, (Ed.), *Sociocultural Aspects of Mental Retardation*, pp. 523–59. New York: Appleton-Century-Crofts.

FINE, MICHELLE (1986) 'Why urban adolescents drop in and out of public high school', *Teachers College Record*, **87**: pp. 393–409.

FRAKE, CHARLES (1984) 'Cognitive maps of time and tide among medieval seafarers', *Man*, **20**: pp. 254–70.

GOLDMAN, SHELLEY and McDERMOTT, R. P. (1987) 'The culture of competition in American schools', in G. SPINDLER (Ed.), *Education and Cultural Process*, 2nd ed., pp. 284–99. Prospect Heights, IL: Waveland Press.

GREGOR, THOMAS (1977) *Mehinaku*, Chicago, IL: University of Chicago Press.

JACKSON, JEAN (1974) 'Language identity of the Colobian Vaupes Indians', in R. BAUMAN and J. SHERZER (Eds.), *Explorations in the Ethnography of Speaking*, pp. 50–64. New York: Cambridge University Press.

HAMMOCK, FLOYD (1986) 'Large school systems' dropout reports', *Teachers College Record*, **87**: pp. 324–41.

HENRY, JULES (1963) *Culture against Man*, New York: Vintage.

HENRY, JULES (1972) *On Education*, New York: Vintage.

McDERMOTT, R. P. (1988) 'The Acquisition of a Child by a Learning Disability'. To appear in conference proceedings on situated learning, edited by JEAN LAVE and SETH CHAIKLIN.

MANN, DALE (1986) 'Can we help dropouts?' *Teachers College Record*, **87**: pp. 307–23.

MIYAZAKI, ICHISADA (1981) *China's Examination Hell*, New Haven, CN: Yale University Press.

MOORE, SALLY FALK (1976) 'Selection for failure in a small social field', in S. F. MOORE and B. MEYEROFF (Eds.), *Symbol and Politics in Communal Ideology*, pp. 109–43. Ithaca, NY: Cornell University Press.

MORROW, GEORGE (1986) 'Standardizing practice in the analysis of school dropouts', *Teachers College Record*, **87**: pp. 242–55.

OFFICE OF EDUCATIONAL RESEARCH AND IMPROVEMENT (1987) *Dealing with Dropouts*, Washington: US Office of Education.

ROHLEN, THOMAS (1983) *Japan's High Schools*, Berkeley, CA: University of California Press.

SELBY, HENRY (1976) *Zapotec Deviance*, Austin, TX: University of Texas Press.

SMITH, DAVID (1986) 'The anthropology of literacy acquisition', in B. SCHIEFFELIN and P. GILMORE (Eds.), *The Acquisition of Literacy*, pp. 261–77. Norwood, NJ: Ablex.

SPINDLER, GEORGE (1959) *The Transmission of American Culture*, Cambridge, MA: Harvard University Press.

SPINDLER, GEORGE (Ed.) (1955) *Education and Anthropology*, Stanford, CA: Stanford University Press.

SPINDLER, GEORGE and SPINDLER, LOUISE (1983) 'Anthropologists view American culture', *Annual Review of Anthropology*, **12**: pp. 48–78.

Raymond P. McDermott

SPINDLER, GEORGE and SPINDLER, LOUISE (1988) 'There are no dropouts among the Arunta and Hutterites'. This volume.

WALLACE, A. F. C. (1968) 'Anthropological contributions to the theory of personality', in E. NORBECK, D. PRICE-WILLIAMS and W. McCORD (Eds.), *The Study of Personality*, pp. 41–52. New York: Holt, Rinehart and Winston.

Chapter 2

Rethinking Dropouts: Culture and Literacy for Minority Student Empowerment

Henry T. Trueba
Division of Education, University of California, Davis

This paper suggests that culture has a critical role in the acquisition of knowledge both at the macro-sociological and at the micro-sociological levels. It is focused on Hispanic minorities, although there are some similarities between Hispanic and other minority groups. Also the paper presents an interdisciplinary approach that enhances our understanding of learning processes within the students' social, economic, educational and political contexts. As in previous studies guided by interdisciplinary perspectives (Spindler and Spindler, 1987a, 1987b; Trueba and Delgado-Gaitan, 1988; Trueba, 1989a), this author explores the educational performance of minority groups and the empowering effect of English literacy in potential dropouts.

According to the US Department of Commerce:

the Hispanic civilian non-institutional population increased by 4.3 million (or 30 per cent) from 1980 to 1987;

the Educational attainment of Hispanics has improved since 1982, but lags behind that of non-Hispanics;

Hispanic men and women continue to earn less than non-Hispanics;

Hispanic families continue to have less total money income than non-Hispanic families;

the poverty rate of Spanish-origin families in 1986 was almost three times as high as that of non-Hispanic families;

the poverty rate for Hispanic families has not changed significantly between 1981 and 1986, but because of population growth, the number of Hispanic families below the poverty level in 1986 was 24 per cent higher than that in 1981 (US Department of Commerce, 1987:1).

The Bureau of the Census, according to the same report, shows a total Hispanic population of 11818 million with 11.8 Mexican, 2.3 million Puerto Rican, 1 million Cuban, 2.1 million Central and South American and 1.6 million other Hispanic. Mexicans constitute 63 per cent of the Hispanics, Puerto Ricans 12 per cent, Central and South Americans 11 per cent, Cubans 5 per cent and others 8 per cent (US Department of Commerce, 1987:2). We do not have an accurate measure of dropouts among Hispanics for a number of complex reasons related to classification problems and lack of empirical data. Some school districts (Los Angeles, for example — personal communication from Los Angeles School District Office) estimate that a minimum of 45 per cent of Hispanic students never finish the tenth grade.

Educational researchers have not been able to present adequate justification for the differential achievement levels of minorities. Some pseudo-researchers have presented unacceptable arguments pinpointing genetic or biological factors as an explanation of minority under-achievement (Jensen, 1981; Dunn, 1987). In contrast, many scholars under the leadership of UC anthropologists have argued that structural and cultural factors (for example, 'cultural ecological theory' along with socioeconomic structural factors — Ogbu, 1978, 1987a, 1987b) can provide an adequate explanation. Further attempts have been made to analyze these explanations (Trueba, 1987a, 1988b, 1988c) and to consider their application to teacher education (Trueba, 1989).

Culture and Failure

Failure to learn is related to communication skills which develop in the context of culturally congruent and meaningful social exchanges. It is not an individual failure; it is a failure of the sociocultural system which denies a child the opportunity for meaningful social intercourse, and thus for cognitive development. As such, academic failure is fully understandable only in its macro-historical, social, economic and political context. Failure in learning is not caused by a single social institution, such as the school or the family (Cole and Griffin, 1983:71).

Both academic success and academic failure are socially constructed phenomena. Failure to learn is a consequence of a given sociocultural system.

> Working within pre-existing norms and role relationships, teachers and students collaborate to create the linguistic and social conditions under which students fail to learn .... Misunder-

standings of one another at that time can lead to assessment of students as less than able or interested learners (Florio–Ruane, 1988:1).

The acquisition of academic knowledge is not necessarily any more difficult than the acquisition of the concrete knowledge required for effective everyday social interaction. Thus some researchers believe that resistance to learning should be viewed as students' rejection of cultural values and academic demands placed on them by school personnel. Erickson (1984) discussed resistance to academic achievement on the part of alienated students in cultural transition. Recent studies on English literacy acquisition have analyzed the use of culturally and linguistically congruent instructional approaches that smooth the transition from the home to the school learning environment (Au and Jordan, 1981; Tharp and Gallimore, 1989, in the Kamehameha Schools of Hawaii and southern California; Delgado-Gaitan with Mexican children in northern and central California, 1987a, 1987b; and Trueba, 1989a, with Hispanic and Indochinese). In contrast, other studies have shown the consequences of the use of approaches which are culturally incongruent or meaningless (for example, Richards, 1987, among the Mayan children of Guatemala; Hornberger, 1988, among the Quechua children of Peru; Macias, 1987, among the Papago; and Deyhle, 1987, among the Navajo). What is significant about these studies is that they show the intimate relationship between language and culture in the adjustment of minority students in the schools.

George and Louise Spindler (1982) and George Spindler (1987), who have consistently viewed education as a phenomenon of cultural transmission — implying the inculcation of specific values — have recently called our attention to educators' need for *reflective cultural analysis* in order to take into account unconscious biases and cultural ethnocentrism (1987b).

In the tradition of the Spindlers' cross-cultural comparisons (1982, 1987b) Fujita and Sano (1988) have compared and contrasted American and Japanese day-care centers, using the Spindlers' Reflective Cross-cultural Interview Technique. They elicited and analyzed videotapes of Japanese and American teachers; then they asked one group of teachers to interpret the behaviors of the other group. This study has permitted us to reflect on the ethnocentrism and projection of cultural values reflected in day-care activities; that is, socialization for 'independence' or for 'nurturing tolerance and cooperation' characterizing respectively American and Japanese teachers. Another approach in looking at academic socialization for achievement has been the one taken by Borish (1988) who uses the Spindlers' model of 'compression and decompression' cycles. He focuses on the socialization of high school Kibbutz young adults getting ready to enter the armed forces who endure intense labor experiences 'in the winter of their discontent'.

DeVos, as a further example, has used projective techniques in combination with ethnographic methods to penetrate complex layers of personality structure and motivational processes (1973, 1982, 1983; DeVos and Wagatsuma, 1966). Suarez-Orozco (1987, 1989), using cultural ecological approaches and projective techniques, shows that the success of Central American refugee children is based on a motivation to achieve. This motivation is an expression of their profound commitment to assist and make proud their parents or family members left behind in war-torn Central America. These research methods have been applied at the broader macro-sociological, political and historical levels, as well as at the micro-structural levels of interaction (Ogbu, 1978, 1987a, 1987b; Suarez-Orozco, 1987, 1989).

The Nature of the Role of Culture in Learning

Culture plays a similar role in both successful learning and the 'social accomplishment' of academic failure, and minority alienation (Florio-Ruane, 1988). Culture provides the motivation to achieve either success or failure. That is particularly true of the ultimate failure of dropping out and rejecting educational institutions, and their knowledge, norms and values. How is this possible? Why is there such a conflict of cultural values? The explanation must be found within the larger sociocultural, historical and political context of minority participation in mainstream social institutions. The indiscriminate use and application of minority group taxonomies (designations of caste-like, autonomous and immigrant types) by cultural ecologists for entire ethnic or minority groups may have objectionable theoretical and practical consequences (Trueba, 1988b:271–87). These taxonomies are based on theories of differential school achievement which do not allow sufficiently for either individual or collective change in status, and therefore tend to stereotype entire ethnic groups. Furthermore, these theories do not explain the conversion of failure into success among 'caste-like' minorities that are described as follows:

> *Castelike* or *involuntary minorities* are people who were *originally brought into United States society involuntarily* through slavery, conquest, or colonization. Thereafter, these minorities were

relegated to menial positions and denied true assimilation into mainstream society. American Indians, black Americans, and Native Hawaiians are examples. In the case of Mexican Americans, those who later immigrated from Mexico were assigned the status of the original conquered group in the southwestern United States, with whom they came to share a sense of peoplehood or collective identity (Ogbu, 1987:321; emphasis in original).

For example, the task of documenting empirically that all or most Mexican Americans were colonized or entered this country involuntarily, or that they have been denied true assimilation into mainstream American is enormous. There is abundant evidence of fairly rapid assimilation of many, while many more continue to arrive of their own free will seeking economic and educational opportunities. Thus, while we can seek in the home culture an explanation for the response of a minority to the academic demands placed by school and society, we must search for explanations that do not stereotype minorities or preempt our search. An interdisciplinary approach may be the solution.

The Cultural Foundations of Cognitive Development

Soviet psychologists, led by Vygotsky (1962, 1978), and Neo-Vygotskians (see references in Wertsch, 1985; and in Tharp and Gallimore, 1989) have provided us with forceful arguments for linking the development of higher mental functions to social activities. Vygotsky viewed language as crucial for the development of thinking skills, and language control as a measure of mental development. His emphasis on the learner's role in determining his/her area of greatest possible cognitive development (or 'zone of proximal development') through culturally meaningful interaction is related to the role that culture plays in communication during learning activities. Wertsch (1987) interprets Vygotsky's position as clearly recognizing the instrumental role that culture plays in the selection and use of specific communicative strategies in adult-child interaction, as well as in the organization of cognitive tasks. Within a Vygotskian perspective learning occurs in two planes: in the social or interpsychological plane, and in the mental or intrapsychological plane. Consequently, the social context of learning is essential to the acquisition and organization of concepts. Within the social context, however, a child learns to use symbolic systems (primarily language) peculiar to the micro-sociological unit in which he/she grows. It is precisely in the selection and interpretation of symbolic systems, also called 'mediational means' (which are culture-specific and culturally defined instruments), that the embeddedness of language, culture and cognition rests.

Wertsch indicates that 'people privilege the use of one mediational means over others' and that 'we need to combine the analysis of collectively organized mediational means with the analysis of interpsychological functioning'. Consequently, if 'choice of mediational means is a major determinant of how thinking and speaking can proceed, then processes whereby groups make decisions (either implicitly or explicitly) about these means should become a focus of our research' (Wertsch, 1987:20–1). In brief, according to Wertsch culture determines or at least facilitates a conscious, collective choice of communicative strategies. Thus if we want to study memory, thinking, attention or other facets of human consciousness, 'we must begin by recognizing the sociohistorical and cultural embeddedness of the subjects as well as investigators involved' (1987:21–2).

Within this theoretical framework symbolic systems are presumed to mediate between the mind and outside reality, and the development of the higher psychological functions is a necessary condition for school achievement. That reality, however, is determined by cultural knowledge transferred from one generation to another and by universal psychological principles which go beyond the individual. Furthermore, both linguistic and social skills are viewed as developing within the micro-sociological units in which children grow, such as the family, school and the peer groups.

Academic Achievement and Literacy

One can argue that effective English literacy instruction requires the transmission of cultural values and skills as much as the academic knowledge associated with mainstream American culture (Spindler and Spindler, 1982, 1987b). The work of Gumperz and Hymes (1964), Gumperz (1982, 1986) and Cook-Gumperz (1986) has forced us to reconceptualize the interrelationships between communication, literacy and culture which form a single symbolic system used in adapting to new cultural contexts and changing with the cumulative experiences in people's lives. As such, literacy is seen as a 'socially constructed phenomenon' (Cook-Gumperz, 1986:1) consisting of culture-specific symbols developed for communicative purposes. As such, literacy depends on the economic and political institutions determining power hierarchies and access to resources; technological, industrial and military complexes not only depend on overall levels of literacy in a given society, but they also determine the quality of instruction in schools and the nature of curriculum.

According to Goodenough, culture 'is made up of the concepts, beliefs, and principles of action and organization' that a researcher finds enacted in the daily experiences of the members of that society (1976:5). However, as Frake points out, the problem is not 'to state what someone did but to specify the conditions under which it is culturally appropriate to anticipate that he, or persons occupying his role, will render an equivalent performance' (Frake, 1964:112).

It follows, therefore, that a good understanding of a culture requires a 'theory of behavior' in particular social settings. In other words, cultural knowledge and cultural values are at the basis of reasoning, inferencing and interpreting meanings. There is an important distinction between cultural knowledge and cultural values in the acquisition of literacy skills. The task is to make sense of text as a message whose content takes meaning within the 'concepts, beliefs and principles of action' alluded to by Goodenough. To accomplish this task we must have knowledge of the codes of behavior (the cognitive dimensions of culture), but also we must share in the cultural values (the normative dimensions of culture) which invite us to engage in communication through text. To see the culture-specific cognitive and normative dimensions operating in the literacy activities of minority students it is necessary to observe such literacy activities systematically and not exclusively in the constrained school settings, but also at home (Delgado-Gaitan, 1989). The following discussion of a research project will help to illustrate the difficulties in creating culturally congruent literacy activities in the school setting, and the advantages of an interdisciplinary research approach.

The South San Diego Writing Project

The South San Diego Writing Project consisted of ethnographic data collected over four years (1980–84) in the San Diego South Bay area along the US-Mexican border (Trueba, Moll, Diaz and Diaz, 1984; and Trueba, 1984, 1987b). The intent was to explore more effective ways of teaching Chicano youth how to write in English. The two high schools selected for the study had a 45 per cent Chicano population and the lowest academic scores in the school district.

High school Chicano students were not only socially isolated in the community and minimally exposed to English speaking peers, but they were also economically isolated in barrios where violence and other gang activities frequently occurred. As we gathered the twelve volunteer teachers who wanted to work in our project, we found out that most of them lived away from the community in which they taught. All were eager to become effective writing instructors and teachers, but most of them felt that students were so unprepared and ignorant that the teacher alone was doomed to fail. Only three of the twelve teachers knew Spanish well.

The objectives of this applied research project, discussed with parents and teachers during an orientation, were to (1) improve the quantity and quality of English compositions, (2) encourage student participation and cooperation in writing activities, and (3) analyze in detail student response to English writing instruction. The specific demographic, socioeconomic and political characteristics of the barrio, as well as the home language and culture of the students, were generally unknown and viewed as irrelevant by teachers. Given the history of low academic performance of Chicano youth in the local schools, teachers felt that students could not succeed in learning how to write in English. Researchers arranged for parents and teachers to meet and become acquainted with each other's culture.

Teachers were asked to organize their classrooms into small groups which eventually became cohesive work teams with full control of their own writing activities. They would explore possible topics, research them, develop data gathering instruments such as surveys and interview protocols, conduct interviews with peers and adults, discuss findings and finally write cooperatively extended and complex essays. The students discovered that writing was no longer a futile school exercise designed by teachers for their own purposes, but a meaningful activity and a means of exchanging important ideas with specific audiences and for expressing their own feelings. Students realized that their individual and collective voices can make a difference in public opinion and in the quality of life at school. Thus Chicano high school students not only significantly sharpened their communicative skills but realized that these skills are a powerful instrument in voicing individual and collective concerns. Teachers would often express their surprise: 'I am impressed. Look!', they said as they shared their students' compositions. A teacher wrote in her diary: 'This [the unexpected high performance of students] was a very successful lesson for me in many ways. It furthers my belief that if what is taught is important in the mind of the learner, much more will truly be learned' (Trueba *et al.*, 1984:131).

The analysis of the project was limited to a theoretical discussion of Vygotsky's cognitive development in the context of writing curriculum, without attempting to account for the psychosocial factors that generated the strong motivation leading to high achievement and literacy levels. To understand the importance of the peer group as a working unit providing moral support during the learning process, especially for young Chicanos undergoing rapid changes at home, would have required more systematic study of the Mexican families' cultural knowledge and values, as well as the processes of integration of school knowledge and values.

Writing gradually became easier and more rewarding to students. Teachers and researchers learned more about students' home life and their aspirations through the English compositions. Then we celebrated our success and enthusiastically assumed the role of 'experts' on writing focusing on technical matters. As one teacher noticed: 'The more controversial and relevant they make the topic, the more willing the students are to write and write well. The more complicated the assignment is, the better the responses' (Trueba, 1987b:246). In our analysis we forgot an important psychological principle advanced by anthropologists, that in order to understand motivation behind expressed values 'one must deal with the universal emotions of love, fear, and hate' and that 'culture, from one psychological viewpoint, is a mode of expressing, in all their complexity, these primary emotions, which are aroused in inner biological urges or occur as reactions to specific outer stimuli' (DeVos, 1973:63).

It has taken several years to realize that it is precisely in young Chicanos' need to express their feelings of love, hate and fear that their motivation to write began to develop. More importantly, this need was most appropriately met within the peer group, because cooperation and team work is culturally the preferred mode of academic activity for Mexican youth. Writing groups offered Chicano students a unique opportunity both to express their collective feelings and to reinforce a cultural value acquired in the home. Furthermore, there was a positive side effect: high academic performance in an English writing class had a positive impact on their overall performance in school, thus stimulating student motivation to produce better English compositions. In the end writing became a vehicle for restoring the credibility Chicanos lacked among other students, and, further, a means for gaining political representation in the school. Violence or other gang activities, low-riding and other conspicuous activities of 'cholos' or 'vatos locos', which had been the common expressions of Chicano youth power, were effectively replaced by writing as a legitimate expression of power, not of brute force power, but of intellectual power to function within the existing social institutions. Here is the essence of empowerment in a democratic society.

Mexican and Mexican American families often find themselves isolated from mainstream society, yet they must face drastic changes in a new world whose language and culture are not understandable to them. Children growing up in these families are subject to high levels of anxiety related to their status as illegal aliens in extreme poverty and their inability to communicate in English with mainstream society. The dramatic change from failure to success in acquiring English literacy cannot be explained in terms of 'caste-like' concepts and cultural ecological theory which would have predicted permanent failure for these students (Ogbu, 1978, 1987a, 1987b). The explanation for the unexpected academic success of the 'vatos locos' rests on their newly discovered meaning of English literacy activities if used for purposes of genuine communication and political representation within the social institutions in which they live, particularly within the school. It was indeed a discovery for the researchers and teachers as well. Writing can become a powerful instrument in the hands of students precisely because it gives them a voice in an academic world in which they have little control of their lives. The recognition, status and personal satisfaction embedded in the ability to communicate well through writing were a joint accomplishment of students, teachers and researchers all working together within the political arena of school achievement. This is how the internal rewards for English literacy acquisition function. The journey from failure to success should help us understand the social construction of failure. The next paragraphs examine an aspect of the social construction of the dropout, the ultimate academic failure.

An Emic Concept of Minority Dropout

The conversion of failure into success is empirically demonstrable, whether we can explain it theoretically or not. Unfortunately, it is a rare event. However, it is important to revise not only the theories of failure and success, but their very components, especially the concepts created by academicians and imposed on students. The concept of dropout is particularly inadequate because it misrepresents the social reality of students' school experience.

The literature does not distinguish the diverse types of dropouts, nor their views of school and reasons for abandoning school within the context of their home culture. Ethnographic fieldwork among dropouts, however, seems to indicate that minority students distinguish clearly different types of dropouts. A study conducted in the San Joaquin Valley (Trueba, 1988a) suggests that Chicano students make conscious and deliberate decisions to withdraw permanently from school for reasons beyond their control (relocation of family, economic need, personal safety, etc.). These students are referred to by teachers as 'discontinuers' in contrast to those pressured to leave school against their will who are called 'pushedouts'. In general, both discontinuers and pushedouts tend to leave school permanently and are presumed by educators to be deprived of the economic opportunities given to individuals with higher educational level. We do not have good studies of the actual outcomes. We know that some of the discontinuers are doing well economically and plan to return to school later on. There is a profound difference between pushedouts and discontinuers with regard to their degree of alienation and their views of school. The cycles of alienation, marginality and illiteracy for some minority students are clearly related to their experience and interpretation of cultural conflict within the school, which are also guided by parental perceptions of schools (Wilson, 1989).

Culture is closely related to the acquisition of knowledge and motivation to achieve, both at the social level (as it affects the family, school and society), as well as at the personal level (as it affects the structure of participation in learning events within specific contexts). The role of culture in students' perception of school activities as enhancing cultural goals and values acquired in the home is instrumental in converting failure into success. But students' cultural perceptions of school as oppressive and as destructive of the home culture can have devastating effects (Wilson, 1989). Therefore, culture must be recognized by researchers as a key factor in the study of minority achievement.

Dropout Research for Empowerment

What should be the focus of dropout research? Where and how should we explore the role of culture in literacy and dropout phenomena? What is the expected impact of such research? Researchers are often overwhelmed with these questions and opt for a detached and safe position; they become 'pure researchers' and reject applied research as unscientific. Others explore intervention-oriented research, convinced that science can also grow from the study of interventions. The work of many anthropologists and psychologists suggests that intervention and explanatory research are complementary and that the dichotomy between basic and applied research was the result of a political and historical accident more than the logical distribution of research activities (Trueba, 1988b:273–4).

Applied and basic research must be conducted in both formal and informal learning settings where students manipulate symbolic systems within their sociocultural environment. The immediate as well as the broader contexts of academic activities in specific learning settings must be studied. They are essential in understanding the organization of behavior and the type of student participation in learning activities. The analysis of literacy activities, for example, and the patterns of student participation should lead us to a more comprehensive view of the 'cultural embeddedness' of dropout and alienation problems. Teachers' knowledge of the home language and culture can be highly instrumental in understanding any communication gaps between the parents or students and school personnel. The school cultural environment and the organization of classroom work should reflect sensitivity to the ethnic cultures of minority students and maximize their participation in learning activities. Minority children can generate their own text materials based on their home experiences as a bridge to engaging in the school culture (Trueba, 1989b). The analysis of learning activities in the home is most important because there inquiry strategies, logical inferencing and cultural congruence occur naturally (see studies by Delgado-Gaitan, 1987a, 1987b, 1989). This analysis can provide insights into possible linkages between self-empowerment efforts on the part of minority students and their parents and the role of school personnel in such empowerment through literacy activities.

Several years ago Erickson called our attention to the need for interdisciplinary approaches to the study of learning:

> Individual cognitive functioning has been largely the purview of cognitive psychologists who have often attempted to study thinking apart from the naturally occurring social and cultural circumstances. The anthropology of education often has studied *anything but* deliberately taught cognitive learning. Clearly, some rapprochement is needed, from the direction of the (more cognitively sophisticated) psychology of learning to the (more contextually sophisticated) anthropology of learning (Erickson, 1982:173).

Empowerment research has developed in the last five years through the integration of cultural anthropology and the Vygotskian school of psychology. Interdisciplinary research on dropouts can become a powerful tool in the implementation of educational reform provided it reflects genuine concern for the culture of minorities. Researchers' understanding of the role of culture in converting minority failure into success is constituted by the following ingredients:

1 compassion for linguistic minority children who are not responsible for their academic predicament and their struggles in adjusting to a new cultural and linguistic environment;

2 commitment to the principles of educational equity, particularly to that of respect for the home language and culture of linguistic minority children;

3 theoretical flexibility and persistence in the pursuit of the elusive role of culture in both the acquisition of knowledge and values both in school and away from school.

The interdisciplinary crossroads of sound research approaches in anthropology and psychology must be inspired by pedagogical principles and a more humane approach to the education of *all* children. The approaches are likely to enhance our understanding of empowerment processes through learning within the context of American democracy and American culture.

References

Au, K. H. and Jordan, C. (1981) 'Teaching reading to Hawaiian children: Finding a culturally appropriate solution', in H. Trueba, G. Guthrie and K. Au (Eds.), *Culture and the Bilingual Classroom: Studies in Classroom Ethnography*, pp. 139–52. Rowley, MA: Newbury House.

Borish, S. (1988) 'The winter of their discontent: Cultural compression and decompression in the life cycle of the Kibbutz adolescent', in H. Trueba and C. Delgado-Gaitan (Eds.), *School and Society: Teaching Content through Culture*, pp. 181–99. New York: Praeger.

Cole, M. and Griffin, P. (1983) 'A socio-historical approach to re-meditation', *The Quarterly Newsletter of the Laboratory of Comparative Human Cognition*, **5**, 4: pp. 69–74.

Cook-Gumperz, J. (Ed.) (1986) *The Social Construction of Literacy*, Cambridge: Cambridge University Press.

Delgado-Gaitan, C. (1987a) 'Parent perceptions of school: Supportive environments for children', in H. Trueba (Ed.), *Success or Failure?: Learning and the Language Minority Student*, pp. 131–55. Cambridge, MA: Newbury House.

Delgado-Gaitan, C. (1987b) 'Traditions and transitions in the learning process of Mexican children: An ethnographic view', in G. and L. Spindler (Eds.), *Interpretive Ethnography of Education: At Home and Abroad*, pp. 333–59. Hillsdale, NJ: Lawrence Erlbaum Associates.

Delgado-Gaitan, C. (1989) *Literacy for Empowerment: Role of Mexican Parents in Their Children Education*. Unpublished manuscript. University of California, Santa Barbara, Graduate School of Education.

DeVos, G. (1973) 'Japan's outcastes: The problem of the Burakumin', in B. Whitaker (Ed.), *The Fourth World: Victims of Group Oppression*, pp. 307–27. New York: Schocken Books.

DeVos, G. (1982) 'Adaptive strategies in U.S. Minorities', in E. Jones and S. J. Korchin (Eds.), *Minority Mental Health*, pp. 74–117. New York: Praeger.

DeVos, G. (1983) 'Ethnic identity and minority status: Some psycho-cultural considerations', in A. Jacobson-Widding (Ed.), *Identity: Personal and Socio-Cultural*, pp. 135–58. Uppsala: Almquist and Wiksell Tryckeri.

DeVos, G. and Wagatsuma, H. (1966) *Japan's Invisible Race: Caste in Culture and Personality*. Berkeley, CA: University of California Press.

Deyhle, D. (1987) 'Learning failure: Tests as gatekeepers and the culturally different child', in H. Trueba (Ed.), *Success or Failure?: Learning and the Language Minority Student*, pp. 85–108. New York: Newbury Publishers/Harper and Row.

Dunn, L. M. (1987) *Bilingual Hispanic Children on the U.S. Mainland: A Review of Research on Their Cognitive, Linguistic and Scholastic Development*, Circle Pines, MN: American Guidance Service.

Erickson, F. (1982) 'Taught cognitive learning in its immediate environments: A neglected topic in the anthropology of education', *Anthropology and Education Quarterly*, 13, **2**: pp. 149–80.

Erickson, F. (1984) 'School literacy, reasoning and civility: An anthropologist's perspective', *Review of Educational Research*, **54**, 4: pp. 525–44.

Florio-Ruane, S. (1988) 'The relation of family, community and schooling in tomorrow's schools'. Unpublished manuscript. Michigan State University, East Lansing, Holmes Group.

Frake, C. O. (1964) 'A structural description of Subanum "religious behavior",' in W. H. Goodenough (Ed.), *Explorations in Cultural Anthropology*, New York: McGraw-Hill.

Fujita, M. and Sano, T. (1988) 'Children in American and Japanese day-care centers: Ethnography and reflective cross-cultural interviewing', in H. Trueba and C. Delgado-Gaitan (Eds.), *School and Society: Teaching Content through Culture*, pp. 73–97. New York: Praeger.

Goodenough, W. H. (1976) 'Multiculturalism as the normal human experience', *Anthropology and Education Quarterly*, **7**, 4: pp. 4–7.

Gumperz, J. (Ed.) (1982) *Language and Social Identity*, Cambridge, MA: Cambridge University Press.

Gumperz, J. and Hymes, D (1972) *Directions in Socio-linguistics: The Ethnography of Communication*, New York: Holt, Rinehart and Winston.

Gumperz, J. and Hymes, D. (Eds.) (1964) 'The ethnography of communication', *American Anthropologists*, **66**, 6.

Graham, D. C. (1937) 'The customs of the Ch'uan Miao', *Journal of the West China Border Research Society*, **9**: pp. 18–20.

Hornberger, N. (1988) 'Iman Chay?: Quechua children in Peru's schools', in H. Trueba and C. Delgado-Gaitan (Eds.), *School and Society: Teaching Content through Culture*, pp. 99–117. New York: Praeger.

Jensen, A. R. (1981) *Straight Talk about Mental Tests*, New York: Free Press.

Macias, J. (1987) 'The hidden curriculum of Papago Teachers: American Indian strategies for mitigating cultural discontinuity in early schooling', in G. and L. Spindler (Eds.), *Interpretive Ethnography of Education: At Home and Abroad*, pp. 363–80. Hillsdale, NJ: Lawrence Erlbaum Associates.

Mehan, H. (1979) *Learning Lessons*, Cambridge, MA: Harvard University Press.

Ogbu, J. (1978) *Minority Education and Caste: The American System in Cross-cultural Perspective*, New York: Academic Press.

Ogbu, J. (1987a) 'Variability in minority responses to schooling: Non-immigrants vs. immigrants', in G. and L. Spindler (Eds.), *Interpretive*

Ethnography of Education: At Home and Abroad, pp. 255–78. Hillsdale, NJ: Lawrence Erlbaum Associates.

OGBU, J. (1987b) 'Variability in minority school performance: A problem in search of an explanation,' *Anthropology and Education Quarterly*, 18, **4**: pp. 312–34.

RICHARDS, J. (1987) 'Learning Spanish and classroom dynamics: School failure in a Guatemalan Maya community', in H. TRUEBA (Ed.), *Success or Failure?: Learning and the Language Minority Student*, pp. 109–30. New York: Newbury Publishers/Harper and Row.

SPINDLER, G. (1987) 'The transmission of culture', in G. SPINDLER, *Education and Cultural Process: Anthropological Approaches*, 2nd edition, pp. 303–36, Prospect Hts., Il: Waveland Press.

SPINDLER, G. and SPINDLER, L. (1982) 'Roger Harker and Schonhausen: From the familiar to the strange and back again', in G. SPINDLER (Ed.), *Doing the Ethnography of Schooling*, New York: Holt, Rinehart and Winston.

SPINDLER, G. and SPINDLER, L. (1987a) 'Teaching and learning how to do the ethnography of education', in G. and L. SPINDLER (Eds.), *The Interpretive Ethnography of Education: At Home and Abroad*, pp. 17–33. Hillsdale, NJ: Lawrence Erlbaum Associates.

SPINDLER, G. and SPINDLER, L. (1987b) 'Cultural dialogue and schooling in Schoenhausen and Roseville: A comparative analysis', *Anthropology and Education Quarterly*, 18, **1**: pp. 3–16.

SUAREZ-OROZCO, M. (1987) 'Towards a psychosocial understanding of Hispanic adaptation to American schooling', in H. TRUEBA (Ed.), *Success or Failure: Linguistic Minority Children at Home and in School*, pp. 156–68. New York: Harper and Row.

SUAREZ-OROZCO, M. (1989) *In Pursuit of a Dream: New Hispanic Immigrants in American Schools*, Stanford, CA: Stanford University Press.

THARP, R. and GALLIMORE, R. (1989) *Rousing Minds to Life: Teaching, Learning and Schooling in Social Context*, Cambridge: Cambridge University Press.

TRUEBA, H. (1984) 'The forms, functions and values of literacy: Reading for survival in a barrio as a student', *Journal of the National Association for Bilingual Education*, **9**, 1: pp. 21–38.

TRUEBA, H. (1987a) *Success or Failure?: Learning and the Language Minority Student*, New York: Newbury Publishers/Harper and Row.

TRUEBA, H. (1987b) 'Organizing classroom instruction in specific sociocultural contexts: Teaching Mexican youth to write in English', in S. GOLDMAN and H. TRUEBA (Eds.), *Becoming Literate in English as a Second Language: Advances in Research and Theory*, pp. 235–52. Norwood, NJ: Ablex Corporation.

TRUEBA, H. (1988a) 'Peer socialization among minority students: A high school dropout prevention program', in H. TRUEBA and C. DELGADO-GAITAN (Eds.), *School and Society: Learning Content through Culture*, pp. 201–17. New York: Praeger Publishers.

TRUEBA, H. (1988b) 'Culturally-based explanations of minority students' academic achievement', *Anthropology and Education Quarterly*, 19, **3**: pp. 270–87.

TRUEBA, H. (1988c) 'English literacy acquisition: From cultural trauma to learning disabilities in minority students', *Journal of Linguistics and Education*, **1**: pp. 125–52.

Henry T. Trueba

TRUEBA, H. (1989a) *Raising Silent Voices: Educating the Linguistic Minorities for the 21st Century*, New York: Harper and Row.

TRUEBA, H. (1989b) 'Report on the Multicultural Bilingual Special Education Program of California State University, Bakersfield'. Unpublished manuscript. University of California, Santa Barbara, Office for Research on Educational Equity.

TRUEBA, H. and DELGADO-GAITAN, C. (1988) *School and Society: Learning Content through Culture*, New York: Praeger Publishers.

TRUEBA, H., MOLL, L., DIAZ, S. and DIAZ, R. (1984) *Improving the Functional Writing of Bilingual Secondary School Students*, (Contract No. 400–81–0023), Washington, DC: National Institute of Education. ERIC, Clearinghouse on Languages and Linguistics, ED 240, 862.

US DEPARTMENT OF COMMERCE (1987) *The Hispanic Population in the United States: March 1986 and 1987*, (Advance Report), Washington, DC: Government Printing Office.

VYGOTSKY, L. S. (1962) *Thought and Language*, Cambridge, MA: MIT Press.

VYGOTSKY, L. S. (1978) *Mind in Society: The Development of Higher Psychological Processes*, M. Cole, V. JOHN-TEINER, S. SCRIBNER and E. SOUBERMAN (Eds.). Cambridge, MA: Harvard University Press.

WERTSCH, J. (1985) *Vygotsky and the Social Formation of the Mind*, Cambridge, MA: Harvard University Press.

WERTSCH, J. (1987) 'Collective memory: Issues from a sociohistorical perspective', *The Quarterly Newsletter of the Laboratory of Comparative Human Cognition*, **9**, 1: pp. 19–22.

WILSON, S. (1989) *Cultural Conflict and Academic Achievement of Cree Indian Students: Perceptions of Schooling from Opasquia Ininiwuk*, Doctoral dissertation. University of California, Santa Barbara.

Discussant's Comments: Anthropology Can Make a Difference

David M. Fetterman
Controller's Office and School of Education, Stanford University

Anthropology is a valuable tool in the quest for equity in American education. Anthropologists are trained to identify larger societal patterns of behavior, including such behaviors as institutional racism. Ogbu (1978, 1987) clearly demonstrates the power of the anthropological lens, using his secondary discontinuity approach. This approach argues that minority groups that were forced to come to the United States (in a subordinate or caste-like role) do poorly in school, while minority groups that made the choice to come to the United States (as immigrants) frequently do well in school. Ogbu argues that subordinate groups' poor performance in school is both 'a reaction and an adaptation to the limited opportunity available to them to benefit from their education' (Ogbu, 1974:12). He focuses on labor market influences and job ceilings for minority groups to explain poor school performance.

Anthropology is also invaluable in facilitating applied work, directly affecting the daily lives of minority groups in the classroom. Erickson's (1984) focus on the role of cultural differences complements Ogbu's societal level analysis. The cultural difference approach states that differences between mainstream and minority cultures result in cultural conflicts that inhibit proper academic achievement of minority youth. The style of interaction, language use, and cognition become the focus of inquiry as well as explanation. They are also useful levers of change for practitioners.

The secondary cultural discontinuity and cultural difference approaches are both useful, addressing different elements of the same problem at different levels of analysis. Arguments suggesting that one approach is better than another, valid or invalid are off-target. I believe that such efforts generate more heat than light.[1] I prefer richer soil in which to plant the seeds of our hopes and dreams: a focus on how anthropology can help us alleviate or solve our most pressing social problems. Ogbu's and Erickson's complementary top-down and bottom-up approaches illustrate the scope of what anthropology has to offer, shedding some light on the school performance of minority youth. Spindler's seminal work in this collection, as well as the works of many others, has also helped conceptualize the nature of the dropout dilemma in a variety of useful contextual frameworks. (See for example Erickson, 1984, 1987; Fetterman, 1982, 1987, 1988b, 1989; Gibson, 1987, 1988; Hanna, 1982, 1988; McDermott, 1987; Ogbu, 1974, 1978, 1981, 1982, 1983, 1987; Spindler, 1974; and Tharp and Gallimore, 1989.) In this commentary, I will draw from my own national research on dropouts to reinforce some of the more salient conclusions by my colleagues. I will focus on the value of anthropological concepts to explore, understand, and change the situation of dropouts.

Anthropological Concepts

The most valuable concepts in the study of dropouts and pushouts include intracultural diversity, contextualization, nonjudgmental orientation, and an emic perspective. These concepts work together in practice, but are separated here for discussion.

Intracultural Diversity

Dropouts are not a homogeneous group. As Trueba states, 'ethnographic fieldwork among dropouts ... indicates that minority students distinguish clearly different types of dropouts'. In my own work, we established a variety of basic classifications, including dropout, potential dropout, and push out. We also recognized the type of students (dropouts) who roamed from one school to another because they did 'not want to get in with the wrong crowd'. Documenting and recording the diversity of expression within the dropout population helps to delimit specific 'treatments'—the application of specifically tailored educational programs and practices to each subgroup or subculture. This approach helps educators meet the individual needs of each student—including the gifted and talented student who often drops out of school because it is boring. During my three-year study of dropouts across the United States, I encountered a handful of gifted minority dropouts. In addition, I found a large number of disenfranchised (but mainstream) dropouts during my three-year study of gifted and talented children (Fetterman, 1988a). Although dropouts are disproportionately represented by specific groups, they come from various ethnic and socioeconomic groups.[2] These differences can help to dispel simplistic stereotypes.

Contextualization

Contextualization is one of the most useful anthropological concepts used to appreciate and understand the dropout phenomenon. 'Academic failure is fully understandable only in its macro-historical, social, economic, and political context' (Trueba, 1989:3). In fact, the knowledge gained by documenting the context of these children and young adults allows the educator and anthropologist to appreciate the group's intracultural diversity, the individual differences that exist within the population. Contextualization is also a useful tool to learn about those who work with dropouts. Trueba highlighted the role of the local context in his study, reporting that most of the volunteer teachers lived outside the school's community and were thus less in touch with their students.

In my own study of dropouts, providing the context for thought and behavior was instrumental in understanding why people acted the way they did. For example, a description of the urban (lower socioeconomic) dropout's physical environment gave policy-makers some understanding about what schools had to compete with in the inner city. A brief description of war zones within schools and such lucrative but illegal activities as pimping, prostitution, arson for hire[3], and various other activities provides some insight into why some students drop out, why some pursue one path over another. I remember one conversation with a dropout in Brooklyn, New York, some years ago. He asked me how much money lawyers made. I told him what the average salary was at the time, and he said that was 'chump change'. He explained that he could make that much in a week from his extracurricular activities, such as arson for hire. For this individual, there was no contest between the rewards of his life-style and what a largely irrelevant and unrewarding academic life might offer.

Contextualizing data can also help the researcher and policymaker appreciate significant gains made by programs for dropouts. During my study, the federal government wanted to close the doors of one of the programs for dropouts because attendance was too low. Former dropouts were attending this experimental program at a 50 per cent rate.

David M. Fetterman

Policymakers compared this rate with the average daily atttendance in the neighboring inner–city school and decided program attendance was too low. I reminded them that they were framing their decisions within the wrong context. These individuals were systematically different from students who attended the neighboring high school. The appropriate attendance rate with which to compare a former dropout's performance is zero. In this comparison, an attendance rate of 50 per cent is excellent. This type of contextual information contributed to my understanding of how much effort these former dropouts were putting into this opportunity. The same information was also useful for policy decision makers; in this case, it provided useful information that contributed to the decision to keep the program operating.

Nonjudgmental Orientation

A nonjudgmental orientation is requisite to describing the complex dropout context. Trueba adopts a nonjudgmental orientation in his discussion about individual academic success and failure, allowing him to see the larger picture — the failure of the sociocultural system. One must put value judgments aside while listening to some dropouts. When a student becomes a drug pusher, his activities must not become the central issue. However one feels about drug pushers, this piece of useful information should not distort one's understanding of an individual's behavior. Instead, attention should be focused on the reasons why the individual entered this occupation. In some cases, a young child is left with few alternatives to support their mother, brother, and sister. This piece of information, like a piece of a puzzle, is critical to understanding complex human actions and interactions. Overemphasizing the lethal effects of this individual's occupation — or glamorizing it — would distract the scientist from putting the pieces of the human puzzle together in a meaningful and cogent manner.

Anthropologists are human beings with biases — often very strong political and personal biases. However, they go to great lengths to make their biases explicit whenever possible. Anthropologists also try to mix their passion for the human condition that they observe and record with a dispassionate conceptual accuracy and detail. In work with dropouts who were pimps and burglars, I had strong opinions about the life-styles of this subculture. However, I rarely let these personal opinions distract me from the task at hand: capturing an honest portrait of the dynamics of human interaction (see Fetterman, 1986, 1989).

Emic Perception

Anthropology's contributions to the study of dropouts rest on the success of eliciting the emic perception. The emic perception is the insider's or native view of reality. Anthropologists usually spend a great deal of time with the people they study, learning their language or jargon, customs, and beliefs. The insights gained from soliciting the emic perspective have already had a powerful impact in the study of dropouts. Trueba accurately reports that recent studies on English literacy acquisition have focused on 'the use of culturally and linguistically congruent instructional approaches that smooth the transition from the home to the school learning environment' (p. 4). Anthropology is one of the few disciplines dedicated to discovering and recording what natives believe — above and beyond any external logical positivist's conception of reality. Verbatim quotations provide a useful demonstration of how the anthropologist attempts to elicit the insider's view. One student who thinks he has been unfairly perceived as incompetent may explain in his own words that he 'is not dumb' and that 'he believes the teachers are prejudiced'. Regardless of whether his view is an objective perception of reality, the ethnographer has shared this individual's unique perspective with us, helping us to understand the motivation for his behavior. People act on what they believe, and those actions have real consequences for their lives.

Like most anthropologists, I strive to understand and record the emic perception of reality. I do not stop when I feel I have reached a reasonable emic threshold of understanding. I step into my emic or social scientific role and try to put all the usually conflicting emic perceptions together to explain why and how miscommunication occurs in a much larger framework. This cultural framework may include a school classroom, program, district, educational demonstration program, or university setting with all its multilevel governmental concerns (Fetterman, 1981, 1988a, 1988b, 1989).

Conclusion

A multitude of anthropological concepts and techniques have contributed to our understanding of the dropout phenomenon. This brief discussion — in conjunction with the chapters of this collection — highlights the value of concepts including intracultural diversity, contextualization, a nonjudgmental orientation, and an emic perception of reality. Additional concepts including a holistic orientation, symbols, structure, and function have also been useful in the study of dropouts. Many of these concepts

David M. Fetterman

and a host of techniques not discussed in this brief chapter are available to practitioners working to understand and improve the condition of disenfranchised youth.

Notes

1 A great deal of conflict is generated from miscommunication and misunderstanding. Trueba's disagreement with the cultural ecologists' approach, in my opinion, generates unnecessary conflict. In addition, while he recognizes that his discussion is limited to a theoretical discussion of Vygotsky's cognitive development without attempting to account for the factors generating motivation leading to achievement, his suggestion that 'empowerment research has developed in the last five years through the integration of cultural anthropology and the Vygotskian school of psychology' is somewhat misleading. Empowerment research in anthropology has a much longer and richer history than suggested. (See action anthropology and advocate anthropology, Fetterman, 1989; Spradley, 1970; Tax, 1958.)
2 Ogbu (1987) presents an excellent discussion about minority intracultural diversity, focusing on nonimmigrant and immigrant minorities. This example was discussed in greater detail in an earlier draft of this commentary. However, it was removed because it overlapped with Gibson's discussion.
3 Arson for hire involves hiring individuals to burn down a building for a fee. Typically, the owner of the building significantly increases the amount of insurance before paying someone to burn the building down. Some students were pursuing a lucrative career in this area during the study.

References

ERICKSON, F. (1984) 'School literacy, reasoning, civility: An anthropologist's perspective', *Review of Educational Research*, **54**, 4: pp. 525–44.
ERICKSON, F. (1987) 'Transformation and school success: The politics and culture of educational achievement', *Anthropology and Education Quarterly*, **18**, 4: pp. 335–56.
FETTERMAN, D. M. (1981) 'Blaming the victim: The problem of evaluation design and federal involvement, and reinforcing world views in education', *Human Organization*, **40**, 1: pp. 67–77.
FETTERMAN, D. M. (1982) 'Ethnography in educational research: The dynamics of diffusion', *Educational Researcher*, **11**, 3: pp. 17–29.
FETTERMAN, D. M. (1986) 'Conceptual crossroads: Methods and ethics in ethnographic evaluation', in D. D. WILLIAMS (Ed.), *Naturalistic Evaluation*, New Directions for Program Evaluation, no. 30. pp. 23–36. San Francisco, CA: Jossey-Bass.
FETTERMAN, D. M. (1987) 'Ethnographic educational evaluation', in G. D. SPINDLER and L. SPINDLER (Eds.), *Interpretive Ethnography of Education: At Home and Abroad*, pp. 81–106. Hillsdale, NJ: Lawrence Erlbaum Associates.
FETTERMAN, D. M. (1988a) *Excellence and Equality: A Qualitatively Different*

Perspective on Gifted and Talented Education, Albany, NY: State University of New York Press.

FETTERMAN, D. M. (1988b) 'A national ethnographic evaluation: An executive summary of the ethnographic component of the Career Intern Program', in D. M. FETTERMAN, (Ed.), *Qualitative Approaches to Evaluation in Education: The Silent Scientific Revolution*, pp. 262–73. New York, NY: Praeger.

FETTERMAN, D. M. (1989) *Ethnography: Step by Step*, Newbury Park, CA: Sage Publications.

GIBSON, M. (1987) 'The school performance of immigrant minorities: A comparative view', *Anthropology and Education Quarterly,* **18**, 4: pp. 262–75.

GIBSON, M. (1988) *Accommodation without Assimilation: Sikh Immigrants in an American High School*, Ithaca, NY: Cornell University Press.

HANNA, J. L. (1982) 'Public social policy and the children's world: Implications of ethnographic research for desegregated schooling', in G. D. SPINDLER, (Ed.), *Doing the Ethnography of Schooling: Educational Anthropology in Action*, pp. 317–55. New York, NY: Holt, Rinehart, and Winston.

HANNA, J. L. (1988) 'Not by courts or schools alone: Evaluation of school desegregation', in D. M. FETTERMAN (Ed.), *Qualitative Approaches to Evaluation in Education: The Silent Scientific Revolution*. New York, NY: Praeger.

MCDERMOTT, R. (1987) 'Achieving school failure: An anthropological approach to illiteracy and social stratification', in G. D. SPINDLER (Ed.), *Education and Cultural Process: Anthropological Approaches*, Second Edition, pp. 173–209. Prospect Heights, IL: Waveland Press, Inc.

OGBU, J. (1974) *The New Generation: An Ethnography of Education in an Urban Neighborhood*, New York, NY: Academic Press.

OGBU, J. (1978) *Minority Education and Caste: The American System in Cross-cultural Perspective*, New York, NY: Academic Press.

OGBU, J. (1981) 'Origins of human competence: A cultural-ecological perspective', *Child Development,* **52**: pp. 413–29.

OGBU, J. (1982) 'Cultural discontinuities and schooling, *Anthropology and Education Quarterly,* **13**, 4: pp. 290–307.

OGBU, J. (1983) 'Minority status and schooling in plural societies', *Comparative Education Review,* **27**, 2: pp. 168–90.

OGBU, J. (1987) 'Variability in minority responses to schooling: Nonimmigrants vs. immigrants', in G. D. SPINDLER and L. SPINDLER (Eds.), *Interpretive Ethnography of Education: At Home and Abroad*, pp. 255–78. Hillsdale, NJ: Lawrence Erlbaum Associates.

SPINDLER, G. D. (1974) 'Why have minority groups in North America been disadvantaged by their schools?', in G. D. SPINDLER (Ed.), *Education and Cultural Process: Toward an Anthropology of Education*, pp. 69–81. New York, NY: Holt, Rinehart and Winston.

SPRADLEY, J. P. (1970) *You Owe Yourself a Drunk: An Ethnography of Urban Nomads*, Boston: Little, Brown.

TAX, S. (1958) 'The Fox Project', *Human Organization,* **17**, pp. 17–19.

THARP, R. and GALLIMORE, R. (1989) *Rousing Minds to Life: Teaching, Learning and Schooling in Social Context*, Cambridge, MA: Cambridge University Press.

TRUEBA, H. (1989) 'Rethinking dropouts: Culture and literacy for minority student empowerment', this volume.

Chapter 3

Culturally Compatible Education: A Formula for Designing Effective Classrooms

Roland G. Tharp
Center for Studies of Multicultural Higher Education, University of Hawaii

'Dropping out' means dropping into something else: the street, idleness, the workforce, or — within the classroom — into rebelliousness, day-dreams or dope dreams. The problem of dropping out is a facet of educational ineffectiveness, and to observe that educationally frustrated minorities drop out most is tautological. Is there a way to make education more effective, involving and satisfying for underachieving minorities? Optimism for a solution is now being generated by the cultural com-patibility movement, which asserts that education is more effective when teaching occurs in a context and process that is compatible with the natal culture of students (Deyhle, 1983; Jordan, 1985; Jordan and Tharp, 1979; Vogt, Jordan and Tharp, 1987).

Some social and psychological processes — developed in the culture of the home and community — are critical to schooling, because schools are organized to expect certain processes. When children possess the repertoires upon which school depends, all goes well; when cultures provide some other set of social and psychological routines, schools and pupils are mutually frustrated. Cultural compatibility researchers have studied the micro-processes of teaching and learning of under-achieving-culture students, emphasized the cognitive and behavioral strengths of these cultures, and introduced changes in schools to make them more compatible with these strengths.

The purpose of this paper is to review some of those features that are important in working for compatibilities. Not all cultural features are equally implicated in educational frustration, and there are differences across cultures in the centrality of features. Nevertheless, some patterns are becoming clearer; and it is suggested that there are two instructional features that are necessary to change in schools for underachieving minorities, no matter what the culture; and that there are four features that have variable effects, and that will produce differences in classrooms depending on the culture. Thus we have a hypothetical (and metaphorical) 'formula' for cultural compatibility: CC = 4V + 2K. Compatibility for a given culture is composed of four variables and two constants.

A major source of the cultural compatibility model has been the Kamehameha Early Education Program (KEEP) group, which over twenty years developed and studied a K-3 language arts program for children of Hawaiian ancestry, in a self-conscious attempt to establish compatibilities (Tharp *et al.*, 1984). The effectiveness of this program has been established in a continuing series of evaluation reports (Calfee *et al.*, 1981; Klein, 1988; Tharp, 1982; Gallimore *et al.*, 1982). Over 2000 Hawaiian children are now educated in classrooms based on the KEEP model.

To test the generality of the compatibility hypotheses, the KEEP group established a research-and-development site on the Navajo reservation of northern Arizona, and has now operated it for six years. Selected because of the sharp contrasts of the ecocultural settings of the two cultures, Navajo and Hawaiian versions of the KEEP program have emerged with clear differences (Jordan, Tharp and Vogt, 1985; Tharp, 1984, 1985; Vogt, Jordan and Tharp, 1987; White *et al.*, 1988). In this chapter I will cite other literature touching on native Hawaiian and native Indian educational issues, but will draw heavily on these data which my colleagues and I have generated at the KEEP sites in Hawaii and Navajo.

The Four Variables: Motivation, Social Organization, Sociolinguistics, Cognition

The four variables that have most consistently demanded attention in the tailoring of classrooms to children are: social organization, socio-linguistics, cognition and motivation.

Motivation

Cultural differences in motivation are central variables in school achievement. Standard school classrooms rely on students' individual need for achievement and individual competitiveness. But Hawaiian and Indian children have higher affiliation than achievement motivation, and a preference for cooperation rather than competition (Gallimore, Boggs and Jordan, 1974).

Hawaiian society is in most settings age-graded, with children largely in association with children, adolescents with adolescents, and adults with adults. Children approach adults only with some form of prior permission or summons, and consequently do not closely monitor adult behavior unless they have some immediate interest in it. Generally, Hawaiian children are much more peer-oriented than adult-oriented. This leads to some chaos in classrooms. The first day of kindergarten, for example, is a considerable challenge to the teacher, who finds no children paying any attention to her instructions. As a consequence, the teacher of Hawaiian children must build his or her own attentional value, by manipulating the incentive conditions of the classroom and teacher behavior itself. In the Hawaiian KEEP classrooms every year the teacher must re-establish herself as worthy of respect and obedience by building a personal, affective relationship with students. The students admire two qualities in themselves, in adults and in teachers: being 'nice' and being 'tough'. Nice is warm and nurturant. A nice teacher must, like a Hawaiian parent, allow the children to 'win' a little and not lose face. Tough is being clear, consistent and unwavering in enforcing her instructions. She must dispense contingently her rewards, such as recess, access to peers and praise. And she must do all this with quiet strength, and without anger (D'Amato, 1981a).

For Navajos, neither extreme of 'tough' or 'nice' should come into play. Navajo adults are highly respectful of children's individuality and of children's sovereignty over their own persons. Any manipulation to control the behavior of others, including children, through such direct confrontational means as contingency management, is considered un-Navajo. While young Hawaiian children require closely contingent rewards and punishments to maintain their respect and good deportment, Navajo children are managed by 'contingencies' of only the most general sort. Expressions of displeasure are made in general terms, without mention of specific individuals or specific events, and take the form of a reiteration of Navajo cultural values.

Navajo society is not age-graded, and children live in close association with generations of adults. Consequently, Navajo children arrive at school already primed to be teacher-oriented (Guilmet, 1978); they visually track the teacher, and attend to slight clues as to her preferences. In both Navajo and Hawaiian KEEP classrooms teachers maintain on-task rates, orderly rotations and excellent compliance. But they do it by very different patterns in their own behavior and in their relationships with the children. The Navajo teachers maintain attention and compliance with tolerance and mildness. Verbal control is infrequent and soft.

We may now turn to a discussion of how Navajo and Hawaiian cooperative preferences can be built into classrooms; and we will see that the exact solution is somewhat different for students from the two cultures.

Social Organization

The social organization of the typical North American classroom is primarily based on the whole, undifferentiated pupil group, with rank-and-file seating and a teacher-leader who gives assignments or demonstrates to the audience. This is typically followed by some form of individual study or practice. Then the teacher organizes some kind of assessment, either recitation or quizzes or some kind of performance. There are other activity settings — such as a small group with the teacher, independent peer groups or individual project work — but they appear less often. One task of educational design is to make the organization of teaching, learning and performance compatible with the social structures in which students are most productive, engaged and likely to learn. For underachieving minorities the typical whole-group organization does not do so.

For example, small group peer-orientation is strong among Hawaiian children and adults, and is deeply rooted in the natal culture (Gallimore, Boggs and Jordan, 1974), where collaboration, cooperation and assisted performance are commonplace in everyday experience. As early as 5 years of age Hawaiian children learn domestic skills and routines and how to care for infants and toddlers. The sibling group, in many activity settings, expands to become a diffuse peer companion group (D'Amato, 1981a), which tends to create its own activities (Boggs, 1985; Gallimore, Boggs and Jordan, 1974).

Hawaiian children have problems adjusting to classrooms that emphasize large group activity settings, in which they are expected to perform independently and orient to a single adult. Hawaiian children do not 'automatically' pay attention to teachers and classwork in large group activities; they do have a high level of attention to peers (Gallimore, Boggs and Jordan, 1974). KEEP kindergartners are engaged in peer interactions 50 per cent of the time, and first-graders 70 per cent of the time (Jordan, 1978). Teachers typically resent these patterns, and condemn Hawaiian children and families as lacking academic motivation (Tharp and Gallimore, 1976).

In the KEEP Hawaiian program the major part of instructional time is spent in small groups. While the teacher is engaged in an intense instructional conversation (Tharp and Gallimore, 1988) with a small group of students, the others are working in groups of four to five, largely on their own recognizance. A peer teaching-learning interaction occurs there every three minutes per child in kindergarten, and in the first grade once in every two and a half minutes (Jordan, 1977, 1978, 1983, 1984).

When the KEEP group introduced this social organization into the Navajo classroom, the same pattern of independent center interaction did not occur. The Navajo children worked independently in the centers, with very little peer interaction. Self-sufficiency of children is not surprising in the Navajo pastoralist culture, where 6-year-olds begin to herd sheep far from home, alone. Certainly peer groups are also a notable feature in Navajo culture, wherever living arrangements are conducive. The groups are formed of siblings, cousins and clan relatives. However, the composition of these groups is typically smaller and less fluid than for Hawaiians, and most Navajo groups are sex-specific; only on rare occasions are girls' peer groups and boys' peer groups mixed (Brady, 1978). Around the age of 8 (third grade) boys are admonished not to 'play with' their sisters, and girls with brothers. In a small community this means almost everyone, since it extends to clan relations. By puberty this is extremely important, and by adulthood male and female roles are clearly defined and separate.

In the classroom peer relationship contrasts between Hawaiian and Navajo were clear. In Hawaii four to five students of mixed sex maximize peer interaction and assistance at a center. Among the Navajo this combination produced virtually no peer assistance. In Navajo the most effective independent groups were composed of two to three students of the same sex, working on the same task. Under these conditions peer assistance was frequent (Vogt, Jordan and Tharp, 1987).

Sociolinguistics

The sociolinguistic features studied in the cultural compatibility movement are primarily the *courtesies and conventions of conversation*. These small features of communication are the molecules of the social organism. While abstract-seeming sociolinguistic variables such as 'wait-time' may seem trivial (Kleinfeld, 1983), these conventions of discourse determine many qualities of relationship, learning and satisfaction. They are the raw stuff of interaction that leads to judgments of rudeness or courtesy, of caring or of disdain. There are critical differences across cultures in these courtesies and conventions.

Wait-time

Rowe (1974) identifies two types: wait-time 1, which is the amount of time given by teachers for students to respond to questioning; and wait-time 2, or the amount of time following a student response before the teacher again speaks.

White and Tharp (1988) investigated differences in wait-time 2 between two teachers of the same class of third-grade Navajo students. The Navajo teacher used considerably longer wait-time than did the Anglo teacher. When a Navajo child pauses, a too-short wait-time 2 by the teacher is interpreted by the child as an interruption. This offends the child, and denies the teacher the opportunity to hear the full student response.

On the other hand, native Hawaiian students have a preference for negative wait-time, a pattern which produces overlapping speech (White and Tharp, 1988). This is often interpreted by other-culture teachers as rude interruption, though in Hawaiian society it demonstrates involvement and relationship. When teachers attempt to prevent this sort of communication, such as by requiring the teacher's permission to speak, or other forms of formal turn-taking, it inhibits participation of Hawaiian children in instructional activities, ultimately silences them, and apparently results in drifting attention.

Participation Structures

In ordinary classrooms Hawaiian children respond in a minimum way when teachers question or address them. Their rich verbal routines, word-play and teasing virtually never appear in classrooms, nor do any long or connected narratives (Boggs, 1985). But when a small group of Hawaiian children are together with an informal, encouraging and participating adult, they often produce group discourse that is co-narrated, complex, lively, imaginative, lengthy and well-connected. The children take turns in speaking, but manifest negative wait-time and overlapping speech. The patterns are very much like 'talk-story', an informal speech-event much enjoyed by Hawaiian adults, in which a group pleasures itself by speaking in much the same way about shared experiences or interests. But elementary schoolchildren are unable to maintain 'talk-story' unless an adult facilitates it (Watson-Gegeo and Boggs, 1977).

KEEP developed the small group instructional-conversation format they call *Center One* to emulate the conditions of adult-facilitated 'talk-story' (Au, 1980; Au and Jordan, 1981). Each day each child meets in a small group with the teacher for a twenty-minute discussion of some text. The group-discussion pattern includes rapid-fire responses, liveliness, mutual participation, interruptions, overlapping volunteered speech and joint narration (Boggs, 1985). These lessons contain more academically productive student behavior than comparison lessons (Au and Mason, 1981).

In ordinary schools for Indian children they too are quiet, abrupt and not verbally engaged. But this is the result of standard teacher-dominated questioning and assessing. The sociolinguistic patterns in Navajo culture are sharply different, where story-telling is frequent, lengthy, and where children listen quietly and reflectively (Wyatt, 1978–79). In councils of almost all Indian groups speakers continue until they have finished, and after a long and unambiguous pause another speaker delivers a fully expressed statement.

The KEEP Navajo program also includes a teacher-led small group instructional conversation (Center One), but the participation structures reflect the natal culture, and thus differ from the Hawaiian. Each Navajo student speaks for longer periods, and other students wait courteously until a clear end is communicated. Then another will take a similar turn. Ideas are developed at greater length, and are often individualistic rather than closely articulated with the ideas of previous speakers. Teachers of Indian children who frequently interrupt narrative events with assessment questions produce a sharp cultural discongruity (Phillips, 1972, 1983; Wyatt, 1978–79).

There are some similarities between the Hawaiian and Navajo groups. Addressing questions to the group at large rather than to individual children allows both Navajo and Hawaiian children to feel competent before performing (Vogt, Jordan and Tharp, 1987) — a recommendation made uniformly by observers of Indian children. When teachers use the 'switchboard' pattern of interaction, Indian children often develop patterns of short answers, interruptions and silence. After years of such interaction, high school students have developed a resentful repertoire of hostility (Greenbaum and Greenbaum, 1983).

Cognition

In seeking explanations for differential school achievement among cultural groups, the most thoroughly investigated patterns of psychocultural functioning are cognitive dimensions.

There is a large body of research detailing the specific cognitive abilities of native Americans. Significant similarities among them — and differences from standardization groups — are reported. These include (1) an overall superiority of Performance over Verbal subscales (Browne, 1984; Gallimore *et al.*, 1982); (2) a superiority of spatial abilities to sequencing skills (McShane and Plas, 1982); and (3) a visual proclivity in perception as well as ability. Indian children do not spontaneously translate their experience into verbal terms, but apprehend the experience as a whole (Berry, 1969; Collier, 1967; Kaulback, 1984; Kleinfeld, 1973; Lombardi, 1970; Shuberg and Cropley, 1972).

This pattern of abilities is different in significant respects than that pattern expected by North American classrooms. For example, writers on native Indian education uniformly emphasize the importance of visual vs. verbal processes in perception and representation, and on holistic vs. analytic processes in thinking, teaching or learning. This is the opposite of regular education, which is almost exclusively analytic and over-whelmingly verbal.

In holistic thought the pieces derive their meaning from the pattern of the whole; in linear thought the whole is revealed through the unfolding of the sections. Holistic comprehension proceeds by incorporating phenomena into ever-expanding circles of context. A holistic pattern of cognition is associated with an entire 'observation-learning complex' (Jordan, Tharp and Vogt, 1985) that includes elements of observing first, and thus gaining competence before performance, learning-by-doing, visual representational structures and children's involvement with adult activities (Cazden and John, 1971; Tharp, 1985).

KEEP has reported that their Navajo children and teachers exhibited a preference for wholeness in many ways. The children clearly preferred — and often demanded — to hear or read a story through to the end before starting discussion (Jordan, Tharp and Vogt, 1985). This is com-mensurate with general native American styles in community story-telling. John-Steiner and Oesterreich (1975) discuss this same phenomenon among Pueblo children, and provide a link from this interpersonal event to a cognitive style:

> Children listening to the many legends of their people learn to represent these visually . . . because they are not allowed to ask questions or verbally reflect on what they hear. They are to say only *aeh hae* to acknowledge auditory attention. As a result, while the verbal representations of some of these legends are fairly simple nursery tales, the inner representations of the same legends, for older children and adults, are replete with highly abstract visual

and symbolic articulations of cultural values (John-Steiner and Oesterreich, 1975:192).

The wholeness itself is a favorite subject of these inner representations. The whole has been symbolized, across cultures and centuries, by the circle. The circle is central in the symbology of American Indians, and its repeated appearance in the Navajo experimental classrooms is another manifestation of holism in cognitive style. The ability of even third-graders to think in terms of holistic form, and their proclivities for circular symbols, was repeatedly demonstrated in the KEEP Navajo classroom. An entry from the KEEP research-teacher's Navajo journal illustrates this point. The Navajo teacher had challenged her 'to try to think of a common story plot as being represented by circular patterning, as opposed to the linear and sequential way I usually diagrammed the plots on the blackboard . . . .'

> After nearly an hour and a half of discussion . . . I managed to represent the events from one rather complex story in an arrangement somewhat like a flower, with petals around the circle of a central problem. The next day I struggled to explain the story in terms of this complex symbol to the students. One of them finally seemed to understand what I was attempting — and suggested that the structure could be represented as a *spiral*, coming up from the center (Jordan, Tharp and Vogt, 1985:34).

This is text analysis on a high level indeed; many instructors would be pleased to have this response from college sophomores.

Holistic and visual teaching strategies include emphasizing whole-story discussions, overarching themes, and using visual diagrams and metaphors. In native American classrooms where the visual/holistic pattern is recognized as strength, and when compatible instructional strategies are used, there is improvement in children's verbal and sequential skills (John-Steiner and Osterreich, 1975; More, 1985). Culturally determined cognitive abilities are not fixed forever; Krywaniuk and Das (1976) have reported significant improvement in sequential memory tasks as a result of compatible instructional programs for Indian children.

In summary, there is evidence that cultural differences in motivation, social organization, sociolinguistics and cognition, when reflected in compatibilities in classroom practices, make for classrooms that are quite different for the two cultural groups. However, there are two prescriptions for underachieving minority groups that are constant: *language development* and *contextualized instruction.*

Roland G. Tharp

The Two Constants

Language Development

The children of cultures that do not emphasize verbal thinking are handicapped in schools because teachers are so heavily dependent on verbal methods, and the goals of school instruction are cognitive skills and knowledge that are largely encoded in verbal and sequential representations. Cultural compatibility educators have repeatedly advocated the use of visual and holistic methods for the teaching of literacy, numeracy and science. However, we advocate with equal fervor instruction specifically designed for language development (for example, Kaulback, 1984; Speidel, 1981a).

Language development at all levels — vocabulary through syntax — must be a self-conscious and ubiquitous goal for the entire school day. Evidence is also strong that language development comes about through use, through purposive conversation between teacher and students, rather than through drill and decontextualized rules (Speidel, 1987a, 1987b). The goal of each day for a teacher should be to engage each child in some instructional conversation, in which the teacher expands, models and otherwise encourages the child's language (Tharp and Gallimore, 1988).

Within KEEP Hawaiian programs, ability in Standard English is the single psychometric variable most highly correlated with school success (Speidel, 1981b). This is unsurprising, since literacy is the single most important goal of schooling. Whether in bilingual or monolingual programs, ability in the language of instruction is both the goal and the major vehicle of schooling, and assisting children to develop those abilities must be a major concern of teachers of all underachieving children.

Contextualized Instruction

The second constant recommendation of the culture and education field is that instruction should be contextualized in the child's experience, previous knowledge and schema. Schools teach rules, abstractions and verbal descriptions, and they teach by means of rules, abstractions and verbal descriptions. Underachieving cultures do not. Schools must assist learning by demonstrations of how rules, abstractions and verbal descriptions are drawn from the everyday world, and how they are applied again to it.

In KEEP's Experience-Text-Relationship (E-T-R) method of reading instruction, the teacher stimulates the students to speak or think of their

60

relevant personal experiences prior to the introduction of new text material (E), and after a period of concentrating on the text (T), the relationship (R) between experience and text is explored (Au, 1979). The E–T–R prescription engages the interest and participation of Navajo children as reliably as it does the Hawaiian.

Embedding literacy, numeracy and science instruction in cultural materials, issues and experiences is quite possible. Contextualizing formal material in personal, community-based experiences is not merely cosmetic; rather, it provides the cognitive links that allow students to grasp literacy, numeracy and science (for example, Wyatt, 1978–79). Contextualization of school material in the life of the child and community expands the schema of the children, and simultaneously captures the social networks of the children in ever-expanding ripples. When the community context is the context of instruction, it becomes more possible to involve the parents, social resources and organizations, the elders and wise teachers of the community in school purposes.

> Successful use of a child's foundations for learning has occurred when the child has not been looked at in isolation, but when education has been looked at as a social process that affects an entire community. More long-lasting progress has been achieved with children whose learning has been explored, modified, and shaped in collaboration with their parents and communities (John-Steiner and Smith, 1978:26).

This approach fosters pride, confidence and a stronger cultural identity, *which leads to native American's greater school achievement* (Gardner, 1986; Huffman, Sill and Brokenleg, 1986). In schools where there is no culturally contextualized instruction, Indian identity is a negative predictor of school success (Chadwick, Stauss and Bahr, 1977). Thus contextualization leads to competence. In the struggle for identity that the minority child must undertake, contextualization allows the child to accommodate to school while remaining anchored in the natal culture — Ogbu's (1982) 'accommodation without assimilation', the bicultural competence on which all workers in the field of culture and education can agree.

These two constants, contextualization and language development, are proposed here as necessary characteristics of all instruction of under-achieving minorities. However, these 'constants' will have very different surface features depending on the particular culture, because the instantiation of the constants is conditioned on the four variables. Language development operations will be conditioned by the conventions of conversation; contextualized instruction will be organized differently depending on compatibilities of social organization and so forth.

The formula of 4V + 2K will produce compatibility, and it will thus produce classrooms that are in major degree specific to cultures. However, one final point must be made. *At another level, the recommendations for tailoring education to the needs of individuals and groups of actual pupils are not dissimilar to those advocated by educational reformers in general.* Elsewhere we have argued that the features listed above are necessary to effective teaching of *all* children (Tharp and Gallimore, 1989). Those concerned with minority underachievement often fail to note that conventional schooling fails to satisfy majority culture members either; the failure of schools to teach adequately is the cause of the current educational reform movement in the United States.

Contemporary schools do very little actual teaching, but instead rely on the characteristic strategy of (a) assign a reading, (b) assess the learning, and (c) give feedback evaluation — the 'recitation script' that has been characteristic of North American education for at least 100 years. Cultures of literate, school-motivated families with verbal-analytic cognitive emphases by and large produce children that can learn on their own from these tasks that schools assign them. In a very real sense standard education relies on the literate homes of North America to provide the teaching of the basic school-relevant skills to students.

But it is *imperative* that teaching be present in the education of under-achieving minority students, for if they do not learn in school, they will not learn schooled skills in any other setting. It is not that there are two types of effective teaching, but there are cultures who prepare their children to learn schooled-skills on their own, and there are those whose children must be taught schooled-skills by the schools themselves.

We have suggested elsewhere (Tharp and Gallimore, 1989) that the rising populations of 'minority' cultures in North America may well force the schools to take on the task of teaching, instead of merely assigning work. We would then see classrooms sensitive to the motivations, conversations, social preferences and thought patterns of their students. We would see classrooms emphasize language development and taking care to contextualize instruction in the meaningful experiences of their students. This would be an enormous benefit to all citizens. There is hope that minority demands for more effective education will save the schools for everyone.

In such a school all would learn, and all would be expanded in their competencies. After all the cultural compatibility movement does not suggest that we teach only to the strengths and for the strengths already present in a cultural repertoire. This would lead to the absurdity that 'white students be taught by verbal methods and Eskimo students by visual methods, a course likely to leave Eskimos even further verbally behind' (Kleinfeld, 1973:355). The reverse absurdity is that since whites are largely taught by entirely verbal means and in competitive settings, they now left behind in visual-figural, metaphorical, holistic and cooperative skills. A higher conception of education is possible: schools where all are taught, and where all learn. Children, their families and their communities would surely resist dropping out of any such stimulating, humane and meaningful place.

References

Au, K. H. (1979) 'Using the experience-text-relationship method with minority children', *The Reading Teacher*, **32**, 6: pp. 677–9.

Au, K. H. (1980) 'Participation structures in a reading lesson with Hawaiian children: Analysis of a culturally appropriate instructional event', *Anthropology and Education Quarterly*, **11**, 2: pp. 91–115.

Au, K. H. and Jordan, C. (1981) 'Teaching reading to Hawaiian children: Finding a culturally appropriate solution', in H. T. Trueba, G. P. Guthrie and K. H. Au (Eds.), *Culture and the Bilingual Classroom: Studies in Classroom Ethnography*, pp. 139–52. Rowley, MA: Newbury House Publishers.

Au, K. and Mason, J. M. (1981) 'Social organizational factors in learning to read: The balance of rights hypothesis', *Reading Research Quarterly*, **17**, 1: pp. 115–52.

Berry, J. W. (1976) *Human Ecology and Cognitive Style*, New York: Sage-Halsted.

Boggs, S. T. (1985) *Speaking, Relating and Learning: A Study of Hawaiian Children at Home and at School*, Norwood, NJ: Ablex Publishing.

Brady, M. (1978) 'Peer group evaluation of narrative competence: A Navajo example', *Working Papers in Sociolinguistics*, 47.

Browne, D. A. (1984) WISC-R scoring patterns among Native Americans of the Northern Plains', *White Cloud Journal*, **3**: pp. 3–16.

Calfee, R. C., Cazden, C. B., Duran, R. P., Griffin, M. P., Martus, M. and Willis, H. D. (1981) *Designing Reading Instruction for Cultural Minorities: The Case of the Kamehameha Early Education Program*, Cambridge, MA: Harvard Graduate School of Education.

Cazden, C. B. and John, V. P. (1971) 'Learning in American Indian children', in M. L. Wax, S. Diamond and F. O. Gearing (Eds.), pp. 252–72. New York: Basic Books.

Chadwick, B. A., Strauss, J. and Bahr, H. M. (1977) 'Indian education in the city: Correlates of academic performance', *Journal of Educational Research*, **70**: pp. 135–41.

Chrisjohn, R. D. and Peters, M. (1986) 'The right-brained Indian: Fact or fiction?' *Canadian Journal of Native Education*, **13**: pp. 62–71.

Collier, J. (1967) *Visual Anthropology: Photography as a Research Method*, New York: Holt, Reinhart and Winston.

D'Amato, J. (1981a) 'Power in the classroom'. Paper presented at the annual meeting of the American Anthropological Association, Los Angeles.

D'AMATO, J. (1981b) 'Sibling Groups, Peer Groups and the problem of Classroom Rapport'. Paper presented at the meeting of the National Association on Asian- and Pacific-American Education, Honolulu.

DEYHLE, D. (1983) 'Measuring success and failure in the classroom: Teacher communication about tests and the understandings of young Navajo students', *Peabody Journal of Education*, **61**: pp. 67–85.

GALLIMORE, R., BOGGS, J. W. and JORDAN, C. (1974) *Culture, Behavior and Education: A Study of Hawaiian-Americans*, Beverly Hills, CA: Sage Publications.

GALLIMORE, R., THARP, R. G., SLOAT, K. C. M., KLEIN, T. and TROY, M. E. (1982) *Analysis of Reading Achievement Test Results for the Kamehameha Early Education Project: 1972–1979*. Technical Report No. 102. Honolulu: Kamehameha Schools/Bishop Estate, Center for Development of Early Education.

GARDNER, E. B. (1986) 'Unique features of a band-controlled school: The Seabird Island community school', *Canadian Journal of Native Education*, **13**: pp. 15–32.

GREENBAUM, P. and GREENBAUM, S. C. (1983) 'Cultural differences, non verbal regulation and classroom interaction: Sociolinguistic interference in American Indian education', *Peabody Journal of Education*, **61**: pp. 16–33.

GUILMET, G. M. (1978) 'Navajo and Caucasian children's verbal and nonverbal-visual behavior in the urban classroom', *Anthropology and Education Quarterly*, **9**: pp. 196–215.

HUFFMAN, T. E., SILL, M. L. and BROKENLEG, M. (1986) 'College achievement among Sioux and White South Dakota students', *Journal of American Indian Education*, **25**, 2: pp. 32–8.

JOHN-STEINER, V. P. and OESTERREICH, H. (1975) *Learning Styles among Pueblo Children: Final Report to National Institute of Education*. Albuquerque: University of New Mexico, College of Education.

JOHN-STEINER, V. and SMITH, L. (1978) *The Educational Promise of Cultural Pluralism. What Do We Know about Teaching and Learning in Urban Schools?*, Vol. 8, St Loluis, MO: CEMREL, Inc.

JORDAN, C. (1977) *Maternal Teaching Modes and School Adaptations in an Urban Hawaiian Population*. Technical Report No. 67. Honolulu: Kamehameha Schools/Bishop Estate, Kamehameha Educational Research Institute.

JORDAN, C. (1978) 'Peer Relationships among Hawaiian Children and Their Educational Implications.' Paper read at the annual meeting of the American Anthropological Association, Los Angeles.

JORDAN, C. (1983) 'Cultural differences in communication patterns: Classroom adaptations and translated strategies', in M. CLARK and J. J. HANDSCOMBE (Eds.), *TESOL '82: Pacific perspectives on language, learning and teaching*, pp. 285–94. Washington DC: Teachers of English to Speakers of Other Languages.

JORDAN, C. (1985) 'Translating culture: From ethnographic information to educational program', *Anthropology and Education Quarterly*, **16**: pp. 107–23.

JORDAN, C. and THARP, R. G. (1979) 'Culture and education', in A. J. MARSELLA, R. G. THARP and T. CIBOROWSKI (Eds.), *Perspectives in Cross-cultural Psychology*, pp. 265–85. New York: Academic Press.

JORDAN, C., THARP, R. G. and VOGT, L. (1985) *Compatibility of Classroom and Culture: General Principles, with Navajo and Hawaiian Instances.* Working Paper No. 18. Honolulu: Kamehameha Schools/Bishop Estate, Center for Development of Early Education.

KAULBACK, B. (1984) 'Styles of learning among native children: A review of the research', *Canadian Journal of Native Education*, **11**: pp. 27–37.

KLEIN, T. W. (1988) *Program Evaluation of the Kamehameha Elementary Education Program's Reading Curriculum in Hawaii Public Schools: The Cohort Analysis 1978–1986.* Honolulu: Kamehameha Schools/Bishop Estate, Center for Development of Early Education.

KLEINFIELD, J. S. (1973) 'Intellectual strengths in culturally different groups: An Eskimo illustration', *Review of Educational Research*, **43**: pp. 341–59.

KLEINFELD, J. S. (1983) 'First do no harm: A reply to Courtney Cazden', *Anthropology and Education Quarterly*, **14**, 4: pp. 282–7.

KRYWANIUK, L. W. and DAS, J. P. (1976) 'Cognitive strategies in native children: Analysis and intervention', *Alberta Journal of Educational Research*, **22**: pp. 271–80.

LOMBARDI, T. P. (1970) 'Psycholinguistic abilities of Papago Indian school children', *Exceptional Children*, **36**: pp. 485–93.

MCSHANE, D. A. and PLAS, J. M. (1982) 'Wechsler Scale performance patterns of American Indian children', *Psychology in the Schools*, **19**: pp. 8–17.

MOHATT, G. and ERICKSON, F. (1981) 'Cultural differences in teaching styles in an Odawa school: A sociolinguistic approach', in H. TRUEBA, G. GUTHRIE and K. AU (Eds.), *Culture and the Bilingual Classroom*, pp. 105–19. Rowley, MA: Newbury House Publishers.

MORE, A. J. (1985) 'Indian students and their learning styles: Research results and classroom applications.' Paper presented at the meeting of the National Indian Education Association, November, Spokane, WA.

OGBU, J. U. (1982) 'Cultural discontinuities and schooling', *Anthropology and Educational Quarterly*, **13**, 4: pp. 290–307.

PHILLIPS, S. U. (1972) 'Participant structures and communicative competence: Warm Springs children in community and classroom', in C. B. CAZDEN, V. JOHN and D. HYMES (Eds.), pp. 370–94. New York: Teachers College Press.

PHILLIPS, S. U. (1983) *The Invisible Culture: Communication in Classroom and Community on the Warm Springs Indian Reservation*, New York: Longman.

ROWE, M. B. (1974) 'Wait-time and rewards as instructional variables: Their influence on language, logic and fate control, Part One: Wait-time', *Journal of Research in Science Teaching*, **11**, 2: pp. 81–97.

SHUBERG, J. and CROPLEY, A. J. (1972) 'Verbal regulation of behavior and IQ in Canadian Indian and white children', *Developmental Psychology*, **7**: pp. 295–301.

SPEIDEL, G. E. (1981a) 'Language and reading: Bridging the language difference for children who speak Hawaiian English', *Educational Perspectives*, **20**, 1: pp. 23–30.

SPEIDEL, G. E. (1981b) *Psycholinguistic Abilities and Reading Achievement in Children Speaking Nonstandard English*, Technical Report No. 91. Honolulu: Kamehameha Schools/Bishop Estate, Kamehameha Early Education Program.

Roland G. Tharp

SPEIDEL, G. E. (1987a) 'Conversation and language learning in the classroom', in K. E. NELSON and A. VAN KLEECK (Eds.), *Child Language Vol. 6*, pp. 99–135. Hillsdale, NJ: Lawrence Erlbaum Associates.

SPEIDEL, G. E. (1987b) 'Language differences in the classroom: Two approaches for developing language skills in dialect-speaking children', in E. OKSAAR (Ed.), *Sociocultural Perspectives of Language Acquisition and Multilingualism*, pp. 239–59. Tubingen: Gunter Narr Verlag.

THARP, R. G. (1982) 'The effective instruction of comprehension: Results and descriptions of the Kamehameha early education program', *Reading Research Quarterly*, **17**, 4: pp. 503–27.

THARP, R. G. (1984) 'The triadic model', in *School Psychology in the Classroom: A Case Study Tutorial*, Minneapolis, MN: University of Minnesota, National School Psychology In-Service Training Network.

THARP, R. G. (1985) 'Wholism and the "Observational-Learning Complex": A Comparative Study of Comprehension Instruction among Navajo and Hawaiians.' Paper read at the meeting of the National Indian Education Association, Spokane, WA.

THARP, R. G. and GALLIMORE, R. (1976) *The Uses and Limits of Social Reinforcement and Industriousness for Learning to Read*, Technical Report No. 60. Honolulu: Kamehameha Schools/Bishop Estate, Kamehameha Early Education Program.

THARP, R. and GALLIMORE, R. (1989) *Rousing minds to life: Teaching, learning and schooling in social context*, Cambridge: Cambridge University Press.

THARP, R. G., JORDAN, C., SPEIDEL, G. E., AU, K. H., KLEIN, T. W., SLOAT, K. C. M., CALKINS, R. P. and GALLIMORE, R. (1984) 'Product and process in applied developmental research: Education and the children of a minority', in M. E. LAMB, A. L. BROWN and B. ROGOFF (Eds.), *Advances in Developmental Psychology*, Vol. 3, pp. 91–144. Hillsdale, NJ: Lawrence Erlbaum Associates.

VOGT, L., JORDAN, C. and THARP, R. G. (1987) 'Explaining school failure, producing school success: Two cases', *Anthropology and Education Quarterly*, **18**, 4: pp. 276–86.

WATSON-GEGEO, K. A. and BOGGS, S. T. (1977) 'From verbal play to talk story: The role of routines in speech events among Hawaiian children', in S. ERVIN-TRIPP and C. MITCHELL-KERNAN (Eds.), *Child Discourse*, pp. 67–90. New York: Academic Press.

WHITE, S. and THARP, R. G. (1987) *Training Handbook for Coding Teacher Questions*, Technical Report No. 41. Honolulu: Kamehameha Schools/Bishop Estate, Center for Development of Early Education.

WHITE, S. and THARP, R. G. (1988) 'Questioning and Wait-Time: A Cross-Cultural Analysis.' Paper presented at the annual meeting of the American Educational Research Association, New Orleans.

WHITE, S., THARP, R. G., JORDAN, C. and VOGT, L. A. (1988) 'Cultural patterns of cognition reflected in the questioning styles of Anglo and Navajo teachers', in D. TOPPING, V. KOBAYSHI and D. C. CROWELL (Eds.), *Thinking: The Third International Conference*. Hillsdale, NJ: Lawrence Erlbaum Associates.

WYATT, J. D. (1978–79) 'Native involvement in curriculum development: The native teacher as cultural broker', *Interchange*, **9**: pp. 17–28.

Discussant's Comments:
Unpackaging Cultural Effects

Ronald Gallimore
Department of Psychiatry and Behavioral Sciences, University of California,
Los Angeles

Roland Tharp's case for the cultural analysis of teaching and schooling is hopeful at the same time as it reminds us of a serious dilemma. Hope arises on two accounts: (1) the demonstrations he offers that native American children can succeed in school provided certain accommodations are made in teaching and instructional practice; and (2) his exciting effort to identify universal principles which can guide efforts to accommodate teaching and schooling to cultural variations.

But his paper also reintroduces a persistent dilemma: how can we achieve educational sensitivity to cultural differences and avoid stereotyping and segregation in a pluralistic society? Efforts to accommodate culture can 'all too easily become the basis for creating stereotypes, and for misjudging the complexity of learning problems' (Fillmore, 1981:24). 'Both the culture of the students and the culture of the school are important in understanding the educational experience of an individual or a group. Nevertheless, a focus on cultural identity may lead to inaccurate interpretations, and stereotyped educational recommendations may then develop' (McGroarty, 1986:304); Ogbu and Matute-Bianchi caution strongly against identifying individuals in broad cultural terms, for fear of *'restricting expectations of academic performance to a generalized analytical category'* (1986:131; emphasis in original).

My colleague Thomas Weisner (Professor of Anthropology at UCLA) and I have been struggling with the stereotyping dilemma, and the product of our collaboration is germane to the task at hand. Our efforts are based on the work of the Whitings (1975), on Weisner's research in Africa and the US (Weisner, 1984) and on our collaboration in Hawaii as part of the Kamehameha Project's cultural research (Gallimore,

Ronald Gallimore

Boggs and Jordan, 1974; Weisner and Gallimore, 1985; Weisner, Gallimore and Jordan, 1986; Weisner, Gallimore and Tharp, 1982).

A Way Out of the Stereotyping Dilemma in Cultural Analysis of Teaching and Schooling

One reason the stereotyping dilemma lives on unanalyzed is the recent history of the disciplines most concerned with culture and schooling. In recent times a flood of micro-analytic research has excited many of us with its promise of identifying specific interaction barriers to the success of minority culture students. Many contributors can be named, but for this piece it serves to mention topics, such as narrative styles, participation structures, differential home literacy experiences and the like. For the most part such work has not treated culture in broad terms, but rather at the level of the individual in specific contexts. Stable interaction patterns, convincingly documented with video tapes and transcriptions, have been treated as cultural in origin, without much concern to identify specifics.

Much has been gained from this work, and my colleagues and I are in great debt. Yet at this same 'Dropout' Conference a persuasive argument by Margaret Gibson reminds we cannot rest content with what has been achieved. Gibson has reported that in the US and other societies there is extraordinary variation among culture groups in their school adaptation and performance. In particular, she has demonstrated that on the question of persistence in school—resisting dropping out—there is astounding variance in the percentage of students remaining through high school, from the low 80s to the high 30s.

Culture at the broad level that Gibson treats it cannot be ignored, in spite of our excitement and satisfaction with micro-analyses. These facts of culture in broader terms must be explained if we are to understand the effects of culture on schooling. If we do not understand why large numbers of students in one group remain in school while majorities of other groups leave, then we can never solve the problem, and perhaps more significantly we can never resolve the stereotyping dilemma. The stereotyping dilemma will remain, as long as all we know is that one culture group stays in school and another does not. The answer of public agencies will be to tailor programs for the groups that stay, and different programs for ones that do not. There is a term for such policies: segregation.

What is to be done? Weisner and I have argued elsewhere (Weisner and Gallimore, 1985; Weisner, Gallimore and Jordan, 1986) that the solution lies in 'unpackaging' cultural effects on individuals. By this we mean linking macro-level analyses of culture, of the sort reported by Gibson, to the micro-level analyses of Tharp and a legion of others. Tharp alludes to such analyses in his paper: He reports sharp differences between native Hawaiians and Navajos in response to independent learning centers. The native Hawaiians display collaborative efforts that correspond to the behavior of the large sibling and peer groups that 'flock' about their closely situated households in a small island niche. The Navajos respond to similar learning centers with more independent work that reflects the activities of shepherding in the vastness of northeastern Arizona.

The principle? The ecological and cultural niche of each group affects the four variables which Tharp identifies as potentially influencing school adaptation and performance: motivation, sociolinguistics, cognitive factors, and social organization. All of this, except for the examples and the research, is familiar enough ground for anthropologists. Few would be surprised by the argument that broad ecological and cultural factors affect individuals. What needs to be emphasized, however, is the prime importance of 'unpackaging' cultural effects so that we can know what aspects of culture effects on individuals must be accommodated, and what can be ignored (Jordan, 1985). This principle is also implied in Tharp's presentation: not all aspects of culture must be accommodated or reproduced for a child to learn successfully and adapt. If not all, then which ones are crucial? With the posing of this question, we are now full circle back to the argument that macro and micro researchers must unite to identify the links between culture, broadly defined, and its effects on individual children. If we cannot separate those that do and those that do not influence school adaptation and performance, we can never escape the stereotyping dilemma. If many, many aspects of culture must be accommodated by schools, then it cannot be evaded anyhow. Is that likely? We think not, and argue our case from work at KEEP (Weisner, Gallimore and Jordan, 1986). What follows is summarized from that manuscript.

At KEEP peer teaching was and is encouraged in independent learning centers in which groups of five to seven children work together. Although the center work is teacher-assigned, adult monitoring—as in the home— is often distal. So long as each child produces, *how* the peer group in a learning center manages the tasks is left to them. This provides the children with considerable latitude, just as in the natal setting (Tharp *et al.,* 1984). Although students are encouraged to help each other, no specific guidelines are enforced for behavior in the peer centers. In a number of evaluations of the KEEP program the effectiveness of the peer learning centers was judged to contribute to the success of the program (Tharp and Gallimore, 1988). But is this effectiveness due to broad similarities between the peer interaction of the learning centers and the sibling interactions so often described in ethnographic studies of native Hawaiians?

In terms of personnel present and types of activities there is little similarity between home and the peer learning centers at KEEP. The ages and diversity of available peer teachers are far more restricted than the natal environment; the emphasis on literacy activities is far greater in the peer centers; and the range of activities available is more restricted than at home. The only compelling similarities between home and learning settings are the absence of direct adult regulation or scaffolding of child performances, and the opportunity for children to engage in shared school work, organized more or less to individual taste. *What is most similar between the two settings is the interaction script involving child-managed assistance in tasks frequently observed at home.* The learning centers provide an opportunity for the children 'creatively' to use a context, relying on self–regulated and mutually regulated sequences of activity — a pattern described as typical of native Hawaiian households (Gallimore, Boggs and Jordan, 1974).

In broad terms these findings (reported in Weisner *et al.*, 1986) supported the argument for selective accommodation of instruction to culture (Jordan, 1985). Not all aspects of the classroom must be familiar to children; and not all features of the peer learning centers must be similar to natal contexts. KEEP found a limited number of similarities between home and school were needed to permit native Hawaiian children to generalize natal skills and knowledge to the classroom.

Unpackaging culture to identify limited, but crucial accommodations is an attractive alternative to the view that classrooms must reproduce an isomorphic representation of natal practices to resolve home/school discontinuities. In addition to the practical problems of an isomorphic solution to differential minority achievement, such a strategy would lead to segregation on an unimaginable scale. Unpackaging culture to identify crucial accommodations offers hope of a middle ground between home/school isomorphism (the stereotyping dilemma and 'resegregation' described by Fillmore, Ogbu and Matute–Bianchi and McGroarty) and neglect of cultural differences in American schools.

To solve the problem of differential minority achievement, and the more specific problem of 'dropouts/pushouts', is no simple matter. Schools require many changes: in social and political support, curricula, standards, quality of personnel, building and materials (President's Commission on Excellence in Education, 1983; Gross and Gross, 1985). The KEEP experience suggests that some cultural accommodations are also needed, although our data are focused exclusively on the early school years. At this point no one can measure the *relative* importance of cultural accommodations compared to other essential school reforms.

But existing research suggests the 'dropout' problem cannot be resolved through cultural accommodations alone. Study after study (see Tharp and Gallimore, 1988, for a review) indicates that too much time in American schools is devoted to drill and worksheets. Even for successful students the routine can be deadening, as it is for many teachers. Little wonder that many who are not doing well anyhow see little point in remaining. To reduce dropping out will require a major change in the way teaching is done. My colleagues and I believe that to discover what those changes can be and how to get them effectively implemented will require the collaborative efforts of researchers, teacher trainers and public school practitioners.

Research-to-Practice and the Droput Problem

The development of researcher/practitioner collaboration was a goal of the Kamehameha Project from its beginnings in 1969. My colleagues and I began to appreciate the importance of the research-to-practice problem in the course of some cultural research in a native Hawaiian community. In 1965 we began a five-year study of native Hawaiian culture and behavior in a community on rural Oahu.[1] Our research included ethnographic and experimental methods, and focused on family, socialization, child development and educational problems (Boggs, 1972; Gallimore and Howard, 1968; Howard, 1974; MacDonald and Gallimore, 1972; Gallimore, Boggs and Jordan, 1974).

In 1968 some of us began to work on the educational problems of native Hawaiian youth at the invitation of the local schools. A plan of attack seemed obvious: (1) use our cultural research base to 'train' school officials about native Hawaiian culture and family life; (2) follow up by consulting teachers as they developed instructional programs that took advantage of the skills and strengths the children brought to school. Over two years various instructional innovations were attempted, based on our community, cultural and linguistic research (Gallimore, Boggs and Jordan, 1974; MacDonald and Gallimore, 1971). Many of these efforts either failed, or had too little effect to justify the cost of implementation. In many instances the innovations could not be sustained after our direct participation ended.

Our frustration could not have been greater. Even with the years of basic research in the community to guide our efforts, we were no more successful than the teachers and administrators we had been so quick to criticize. Our studies of Hawaiian culture seemed relevant, but we were unable to translate the findings into workable, effective and stable changes in classroom practices. But from these initial efforts we did learn some important lessons, one of which was the daunting nature of translating research into effective practice. We have naively assumed that solutions could be devised by direct extrapolation from research to the classroom. Although we had spent many hours observing in schools, none of us had actually worked in the classroom, or tried to teach Hawaiian students with the approaches we had extrapolated from cultural studies. Our relationship to teachers and students alike had been relatively distant, and though involved in the schools, we were not truly part of schools operations. The innovations that seemed so appealing and workable in the seminar room did not easily translate into workable, reliably implemented instructional practices. We knew how to do research. The teachers knew how to run a classroom. But none of us knew how to combine both kinds of knowledge and skill. A bridge was needed between research and practice.

We needed a situation in which we could collaborate with practising teachers, try out and closely watch innovations, apply the tools of science, learn from our mistakes and keep working on a problem until we solved it. Researchers and practitioners had to share responsibility and risk over time. It was recognition of this step between research and practice that led to the creation of the Kamehameha Early Education Project, and which was an important factor in whatever success was achieved.

Neither the KEEP program nor any other is a panacea for the dropout problem or other mutual problems of the schools and cultural minorities. Indeed, the program developed at KEEP may be less important than the broader lesson: to deal with problems such as dropouts will require, as part of the mix, sufficient attention to the problem of translating research into practice, including the creation of researcher/practitioner collaboration.

Principles of Researcher/Practitioner Collaboration

There are many barriers which hinder development of long-term researcher/practitioner collaboration. Institutional arrangements are lacking which permit collaboration of university and public school personnel. Younger university faculty cannot afford to do such work because it is less valued, and because the interval between initiation and publication is sometimes long, and the chances of success low. Funds for such research are minimal. The public schools have no mechanisms readily available for collaboration with researchers, and may perceive such efforts as disruptive or threatening. Even when innovations are successfully developed, implemented and tested in one site, the traditional methods of coursework and workshops are often ineffective means of dissemination and diffusion.

What does it require to overcome these barriers and achieve researcher/practitioner collaboration? Roland and I (Tharp and Gallimore, 1979, 1982) have tried to extract some principles. Long-term collaboration requires conditions not often available, including longevity and stability of funding. Stable, long-term funding is not simply desirable, it is an indispensable requirement for the kind of work which is needed to solve the dropout problem. But long-term funding need not be of large magnitudes; we have been experimenting recently with 'KEEP-like' collaboration, funded largely out of the personal commitments of university researchers and public school personnel, aided by small sums of money for equipment, tapes and transcription. In these cases the stability of funding is provided by the university in the form of tenured professorships which include an expectation of continued research and publication, and the cooperation of local schools which give teachers time for staff development. The latter resource can be devoted to study of a problem in collaboration with a university researcher over an extended period; the results of such research are acquired by the participating teachers and shared with others through normal in-service arrangements.

A problem-driven focus is an effective way to maintain researcher-practitioner collaboration over a long period. The problem must be chosen carefully: it becomes the organizing dynamic which integrates researchers and practitioners. A key element is evaluation pressure. This means that the researchers must share responsibility on the same terms as the practitioners. The solitude of academia and its comforting abstractions are not options for the teachers and students. To make a difference, researchers must share the dismal moments, and an effective means to achieve such sharing is to subject everyone involved to the same evaluation pressures.

Working in a school over an extended period is a humbling experience. Translating research into practice calls for skepticism, self-criticism and a willingness to base decisions on data. The last is the hardest of all. Teachers find it difficult to confront negative results when they have put their best into an effort. This experience may be more familiar to researchers, but it is never pleasant. In response to a failing innovation, there is a strong tendency to discount the data, the methods and even the idea of evaluating — it is easy to be convinced that because the parents, children and/or staff like some program element it must be good. Again and again at KEEP we had to rally the team to continue, to start again, to try another approach, to refine our methods and to learn from mistakes and failure. Sometimes we had to do more research, or abandon favorite hypotheses. Without the continuity of collaboration for some years, neither the program nor the results would have been possible.

The task of problem-driven research is not to test theories. It is to solve problems. But this does not eliminate the possibility of theory-related research. Indeed, many theories have proved helpful, and out of the clash of ideas have come data of theoretical importance. Visitors to KEEP often commented on the conflicting conceptions and understandings that team members had of the same phenomena. This complexity arose from the complexity of the phenomena with which we had to deal—we were working with real children and teachers in a real school. A single perspective was not sufficient—neither was a single method.

Ethnographic and qualitative methods played a major role throughout the KEEP work, but they were not enough. At crucial times careful experiments contributed to the process, and in the end a vitally important step was a full-scale evaluation with random assignment to treated and untreated conditions. However, for many researchers it may prove disconcerting to learn that powerful quantitative techniques have limited uses in a research-to-practice enterprise. Much less tidy measures must be in the mix if we are to understand and deal with the subtle and complex factors that confront minority children in the public schools.

In a cooperative atmosphere, and over time (the longevity factor again), diversity of theory and method generates better outcomes. Certain to fail are efforts that are so narrowly focused in a disciplinary sense that they cannot deal with real-life complexities. Any effort to study and modify teaching and school practices will fail if it is approached from a single perspective, whether that is anthropology, sociolinguistics, social psychology or the effective teaching paradigm.

Professors and researchers have much to learn if their studies and findings are to have an impact on public school practices. One of the most important of these is the limitations of the university 'culture of teaching' as a source of consulting tools for working in public schools. In the beginning we assumed, as many of our colleagues did, that change in schools can be achieved through 'lectures and reprints'. At KEEP this was jokingly referred to as the 'reprint theory of change'. Such assumptions about how to assist others are so much a part of university/research culture that they, like features of any culture, are transparent. Lectures and reprints are of marginal value in using research to achieve change in public school practices. Until the university attends to its theories and assumptions of assisting performance of teachers and schools, I fear little will change. But attacking this problem, like so many others, includes the two elements needed to sustain researcher/teacher collaboration. Those who study competing theories of assisting teachers and schools will no doubt help those they study, but also make discoveries worth publishing for other researchers.

Note

1 The Hawaiian Community Research Project (HCRP) was organized by the Princess Bernice Pauahi Bishop Museum, which has a long tradition of conducting anthropological research in Polynesia. From 1965 to 1970 the HCRP was supported by grants from the National Institute of Mental Health and the State of Hawaii. Additional support was provided by the Department of Psychology and Social Sciences Research Institute, University of Hawaii.

References

BOGGS, S. T. (1972) 'The meaning of questions and narratives to Hawaiian children', in C. B. CAZDEN, V. P. JOHN, and D. HYMES, (Eds.), *Functions of language in the classroom*, pp. 299–327. New York: Teachers College Press.

FILLMORE, LILY WONG (1981) 'Cultural perspectives on second language learning,' *TESL Reporter*, **14** (2): pp. 23–31.

GALLIMORE, RONALD and HOWARD, ALAN (Eds.) (1968) *Studies in a Hawaiian Community: Na Makamaka O Nanakuli*, Pacific Anthropological Records, No. 1. Honolulu: Department of Anthropology, Princess Bernice Pauahi Bishop Museum.

GALLIMORE, RONALD, BOGGS, JOAN WHITEHORN and JORDAN, CATHIE (1974) *Culture, Behavior, and Education: A Study of Hawaiian-Americans*, Beverly Hills, CA: Sage Publications.

GROSS, BERNICE and GROSS, RONALD (Eds.) (1985) *The Great School Debate: Which Way for American Education?* New York: Simon and Schuster.

HOWARD, ALAN (1974) *Ain't No Big Thing: Coping Strategies in a Hawaiian-American Community*, Honolulu: University of Hawaii Press.

JORDAN, CATHIE (1985) 'Translating culture: From ethnographic information to educational program,' *Anthropology and Education Quarterly*, **16**, 2: pp. 106–23.

MACDONALD, S. and GALLIMORE, R. (1971) *Battle in the Classroom*, Scranton, PA: Intext Educational Publishers.

MACDONALD, SCOTT and GALLIMORE, RONALD (1972) *Battle in the Classroom: Innovations in Classroom Techniques*, Scranton, PA: Intext Educational Publishers.

MCGROARTY, MARY (1986) 'Educator's response to sociocultural diversity: Implications for practice.' in Bilingual Education Office, California State Department of Education (Eds.), *Beyond Language: Social and Cultural Factors in Schooling Language Minority Students*, pp. 299–343. Los Angeles, CA: California: State University, Los Angeles. Evaluation, Dissemination and Assessment Center.

OGBU, JOHN U. and MATUTE-BIANCHI, MARIA EUGENIA (1986) 'Understanding sociocultural factors: Knowledge, identity, and school adjustment', in Bilingual Education Office, California State Department of Education (Eds.) *Beyond Language: Social and Cultural Factors in Schooling Language Minority Students,* pp. 73–142. Los Angeles, CA: California State University, Los Angeles.

PRESIDENT'S COMMISSION ON EXCELLENCE IN EDUCATION (1983) *A Nation at Risk,* Washington, DC: Government Printing Office.

THARP, ROLAND G. and GALLIMORE, RONALD (1979) 'The ecology of program research and evaluation: A model of evaluation succession', in LEE SECHREST (Ed.), *Evaluation Studies Review Annual*, No. 4, pp. 39–60. Beverly Hills, CA: Sage Publications.

THARP, ROLAND G. and GALLIMORE, RONALD (1982) 'Inquiry process in program development,' *Journal of Community Psychology*, **10**: pp. 103–18.

THARP, ROLAND G. and GALLIMORE, RONALD (1988) *Teaching Mind and Society: A Theory of Teaching, Literacy and Education*, Cambridge: Cambridge University Press.

THARP, ROLAND G. *et al.* (1984) 'Product and process in applied developmental research: Education and the children of a minority,' in MICHAEL E. LAMB, ANN L. BROWN and BARBARA ROGOFF (Eds.), *Advances in Developmental Psychology*. Vol. 3, pp. 91–141. Hillsdale, NJ: Lawrence Erlbaum Associates.

WEISNER, THOMAS S. (1982) 'Sibling interdependence and child caretaking: A cross-cultural view,' in M. LAMB and B. SUTTON-SMITH (Eds.), *Sibling Relationships: Their Nature and Significance across the Lifespan*. Hillsdale, NJ: Lawrence Erlbaum Associates.

WEISNER, THOMAS S. (1984) 'Ecocultural niches of middle childhood: A cross-cultural perspective,' in W. ANDREW COLLINS (Ed.), *Development during Middle Childhood: The Years from Six to Twelve*, pp. 335–69. Washington, DC: National Academy of Sciences Press.

WEISNER, THOMAS S., GALLIMORE, R. and JORDAN, C. (1982) *Demographic Description of KEEP Families in Cohorts I through V, by Sample Source and Cohort*, Technical Report No. 99, Honolulu: Kamehameha Schools/Bishop Estate, Kamehameha Early Education Program.

WEISNER, THOMAS S. and GALLIMORE, RONALD (1985) 'The Convergence of Ecocultural and Activity Theory'. Paper read at the annual meeting of the American Anthropological Association, Washington, DC.

WEISNER, THOMAS S., GALLIMORE, RONALD and JORDAN, CATHIE (1982) *Demographic Description of KEEP Families in Cohorts I through V, by Sample Source and Cohort*. Technical Report No. 99. Honolulu: Kamehameha Early Education Program.

WEISNER, THOMAS S., GALLIMORE, RONALD and THARP, ROLAND G. (1982) 'Concordance between ethnographer and folk perspectives: Observed performance and self-ascription of sibling caretaking roles,' *Human Organization*, **41**, 3: pp. 237–44.

WEISNER, THOMAS S., GALLIMORE, RONALD and JORDAN, CATHIE (1986) *Unpackaging Cultural Effects on Classroom Learning: Hawaiian Peer Assistance and Child-generated Activity*, Los Angeles: University of California, Department of Psychiatry & Biobehavioral Sciences.

WHITING, B. and WHITING, J. (1975) *Children of Six Cultures*, Cambridge, MA: Harvard University Press.

Chapter 4

Mario, Jesse and Joe: Contextualizing Dropping Out

Perry Gilmore and David Smith
University of Alaska, Fairbanks

Last month in Alaska The Governor's Interim Commission on Children and Youth issued a widely circulated report on the status of young people in the state (January, 1988). Prefacing the report with the assertion that 'this generation is at risk' because 'they are falling behind their peers nationally', the commission reviewed a number of serious problems for Alaskan youth. Among these is the very high dropout rate. Only two-thirds of Alaskan youth are graduated by the age of 18. The dropout rate for native youth is several times that for non-native. The report goes on to remind us that dropouts serve more time in jail, more often are into substance abuse, are less employable and have lower paying jobs than do those who graduate from high school. The report concludes that dropping out is a serious drain on the state's social and financial resources and recommends a series of steps to deal with the problem. All of the solutions are designed to find ways to *keep children in schools*.

This is not a particularly remarkable report; it is, in fact, fairly typical. It reflects four commonly held characteristics of a popular view of dropping out: (1) framing the phenomenon as a serious social problem; (2) focusing on the inadequacy of schooling practices; (3) implying a causal relationship between dropping out and other social ills; and (4) seeing the solution as keeping kids in school. It is our contention that this characteristic popular view cannot adequately account for or explain school dropouts. Further, as a model for analysis and reform, such a framework can obfuscate the salient features of the dropout phenomenon and lead to educational 'improvements' which tend to intensify rather than ameliorate the problems. Anthropological criticisms of basing research and reform on such popular paradigms have been detailed elsewhere at length; for example, McDermott and Hood (1982) make the argument with respect to school failure, and Smith (1983, 1985, 1986) has made parallel arguments critiquing popular views of illiteracy.

Over the last two decades educational anthropologists, guided by the popular press, the educational research community and the educational reformers, have focused their efforts on three successive topics: minority school failure, growing national illiteracy rates and most recently high school dropouts. By focusing on these as separate topics we may have at times convinced ourselves and our audiences that these were truly disparate phenomena rather than related manifestations of an intricate web of cultural circumstances. In this chapter we attempt to build on the knowledge generated by our own anthropological studies of literacy and apply that set of socio-cultural understanding to the investigation of the dropout phenomenon. In the following discussion we develop and illustrate two major themes emerging from a view which seeks to understand and account for social phenomena such as dropping out, or minority school failure and illiteracy, by first adequately contextualizing them. Several examples will be drawn from our research in black and Hispanic communities in urban west Philadelphia and native Alaskan Indian and Eskimo ethnic populations in rural and urban settings in Alaska.

First, we will argue that dropping out is best accounted for by seeing it not as a function of schooling and in particular how schooling is done, but by an understanding of what 'dropping out' means in the lives of the individuals who leave school. The second theme we will examine is that dropping out is not a single phenomenon. The popular monolithic view fails to recognize the complex range and variation of the nature, functions and meanings of the actual behavior. The gloss itself, 'dropping out', suggests a set of assumptions about both the actors and the act as well as the situation or place being dropped out of, which we question.

We have attempted to illustrate the significance of this contextualized perspective of dropping out in the title of our paper. Mario, Gary, Jesse and Joe are not case studies from Philadelphia or Alaska but refer instead to Mario Cuomo, Gary Hart, Jesse Jackson and Joe Biden. For each of these individuals their relationship to the presidential race and specifically the primary race is very different, representing a range of strategies with various possible outcomes. At the time we wrote the abstract for this paper Cuomo had not declared his candidacy although many believed that the Democratic nomination was his for the asking; Hart had been in and out and in again; Jackson was running hard, but because he was black few pundits were giving him much chance; and Biden had dropped out and apparently given up. Dropping out, staying in or never entering the primaries is not necessarily a good predictor of performance in 'the race' itself. Without laboring the parallels, it is not difficult to see reflections of possible student school biographies in each of the candidates' (or non-candidates') primary histories. In the case of schooling, dropping out is best accounted for by seeing it not as a function of schooling but by an understanding of 'the race' itself—the larger cultural frame.

The Finger or the Moon: Seeing the Larger Cultural Context

Michelle Fine presents statistics that shock us into contextualizing dropping out of school. In the affluent sections of New York City white students who drop out of high school have an employment rate of 43 per cent. In the poor areas of the City the employment rate for minority graduates is 33 per cent (Fine, 1985).

On one of the smaller islands of Hawaii a Japanese father, in discussing his son's school problems with the boy's teacher, expressed this contextualized view more poetically:

> Education is like the finger. For the child who does not know of the moon, one raises the finger to point to the moon. The finger and the moon are not the same. If by means of the finger the child sees the moon, then the finger drops away. If, however, the child's eyes become stuck on the finger and he never goes past it, then the finger becomes a hindrance to knowing the moon (Horikawa, 1987:6).

This relationship between means and ends is a crucial consideration. As his father cautions, school and life's knowledge are not the same. The challenge to educators then becomes not simply how to prevent dropping out of school but to understand under what conditions the 'finger' is important, when it has become a hindrance and when it is irrelevant to seeing the 'moon'. (With respect to this last point, it could be argued that Mario Cuomo, who has not officially entered and thus has not participated in the Democratic primaries, may well be as deeply in the presidential race as any of the declared candidates. He may well recognize that the goal is the 'moon', hoping the others fixation on the 'finger' will prove a hindrance.)

Michael Bopp, primary author of the Four Worlds Program and a founder of the Kipohtakaw Education Centre on the Alexander Reserve in Alberta, voices this same sentiment in arguing for holistic, community controlled educational programs for native Americans, 'Actually, schooling is a second-order problem. The primary problem is life itself, and the way life is being led' (Bopp, 1986:3). (It is worth noting in passing that the Kipohtakaw program was developed, in part, in response to a 100 per cent dropout rate on the reserve. After five years of the holistic program dropping out was virtually eliminated.)

The examples used later in this paper make the point that if we raise our gaze from schooling as an a priori bounded entity, and look at academic careers in the larger context of 'life itself, and the way life is being led', we will be driven to relocate the causes, the meanings and ultimately the problematicity of dropping out. It is fundamentally not a problem of schooling and can never be addressed by simply tinkering with the way we do schooling. This is seen in the relationship between various academic career paths and life contexts as well as in the overt, out-of-school political strategies explicitly and implicitly demanded for school success.

When Is Dropping Out: Range and Variation

The second theme to emerge from the histories we have examined is that dropping out is not a single phenomenon. While Michelle Fine (1986) has convincingly demonstrated that dropping out of a black metropolitan high school may be an explicit strategy for resisting the imposition of an oppressive political agenda or for escaping the irresolvable contradictions of society, this may be little related to dropping out of an Alaskan village school to pursue a subsistence life-style. Not only does a monolithic view fail to recognize crucial differences in the meanings of dropping out; it is equally inadequate for seeing instructive connections between apparently unrelated phenomena (for example, the variety of strategies needed for staying in school, college drop out patterns, and even adult schooling issues). With respect to adult schooling Smith (1985) notes that participation in an adult literacy center was seen as a search for redemption from the social opprobrium of dropping out rather than remediation.

Consider, for example, the fact that most of our statistics on dropping out do not capture subsequent events in the lives of the dropout. In the Governor's report mentioned at the opening of this paper it was stated that only two-thirds of the state's 18-year-olds are graduated from high school. What can be misleading about this figure is that half of those who do not graduate return for a GED at some later time. What is glossed as dropping out might more accurately be described as taking time out or taking an alternative and often less painful route. Consider those who stay in school in special education tracks and the like. They may graduate but essentially without the equivalent of a high school education. These individuals have in effect dropped out by staying in.

The contextualized view of dropping out adopted here is self-evident to anthropologists. While we would assume that surface differences or similarities have little to do with underlying reality, educators are seldom encouraged by training or given the room in practice to take this stance. As a result, our insights too often remain essentially ours and we are viewed as impractical. Or worse, by arguing that the problems of schooling are located in the larger society and cannot be solved through identifying and directly addressing those individuals at risk, we are faced with the dilemma of seeming to advocate a position that dooms the disenfranchised who must content with the present reality of schooling.

The challenge before us, becomes not simply to vindicate our science, but to demonstrate how these insights may routinely be incorporated into educational policy and practice. In the following section we describe a few cases which like the candidates mentioned in the title have unique and varied experiences as they cope with different patterns of staying in and dropping out. The contextualized and varied circumstances presented for each begin to describe a different understanding of dropping out. Just as they point to a new conceptualization of the issue, they suggest a new framework for action.

Portraits: Some Strategies for Staying In, Dropping Out or Recontextualizing School Participation

We regularly hear talk about students dropping out as if it was a totally independent action—a choice, even if a misguided one, which is considered and carried out. What we will consider in the following examples are ways in which the schools benignly arrange for this to happen. A range of ethnographic research has suggested that tracking, sorting and labeling are means to this end (for example, Rist, 1970; Goldman, 1982; Collins, 1987; Gilmore, 1982; Ogbu, 1987). Done with often the best of intentions, that is to provide appropriate 'help', students find themselves assigned and ascribed to low tracks and special education classes which maximize the likelihood of school failure, low literacy achievement and dropping out of school. Further, once ascribed to the track, there is little opportunity to switch tracks, be reassessed unbiasedly or literally 'escape'. The low track path through school tends to be a shorter one. It generally leads to an early exit from school A more fitting descriptive label for the practice of leaving school before graduation might be 'tracked out' or 'pushed out' rather than 'dropped out'.

In Gilmore's (1982) three-year literacy study in a low income black urban community, a special high track class, referred to as the Academics

Plus Program, is describ̄d. The selection process for this elementary school program was in effect a preliminary stage in a systematic process of preparing students to stay in or drop out of school years later. The criterion for selection in the west Philadelphia program considered a range of student characteristics including academic achievement, IQ test scores, 'cooperative attitude' and the like. Less than a third of the student population was selected for admission to the Academics Plus Program. Though the program did not guarantee general school success, it certainly maximized the chances for it. Those not selected were selected for something else, although that was never stated as such. They were effectively selected to be 'at risk', in both the euphemistic and the physical sense. Being placed in a low track in this particular study site meant that you would have to attend 'tougher' middle schools which were frequently in neighborhoods considered to be unsafe. Beyond the obvious academic risks, the physical and psychological risks were a visceral daily reality.

The students selected for the high track classes had the promise of possible acceptance in the various specialized magnet schools at the middle school and high school levels. These schools were generally perceived to offer a higher quality of education, more challenging curriculum and higher caliber of teaching faculty. The schools were more desegregated ethnically, racially and economically. If parents were at all aware of the consequences at that first selective crossroad in terminal tracking, they were concerned that their children be chosen for the track that would keep the gates open for possible success. We tend to focus on dropping out by looking to 16-year-olds in high school who are about to make that decision. Yet these mothers knew at some level that the track assigned to their children in the fourth grade would be a key factor six years later. Some mothers simply cried as they turned to walk out of the door, holding their youngster close, heads bowed in deference to the sentence that had been pronounced.

One mother we worked with in the community (Mrs R.) had four children go through the school in the study site. Three of her children had gone through the selection and assessment process successfully. The three were all in magnet schools and doing extremely well. Mrs R. had a history of commitment and involvement at the school. She had been an aid in the library and classrooms, a president of the Parent Teachers Association and a loyal supporter of the school's principal. When her youngest child was in the fourth grade, the bad news came. He did not qualify for a recommendation to the magnet school which his siblings attended. The teacher explained that his grades in third grade had not been good and, though he was doing better in her class, the evaluation was to be based on the third grade performance. Mrs R. argued that he had had difficulty with the teacher the year before, who was a first-year teacher with some obvious weaknesses. The teacher was adamant: the boy did not qualify.

Mrs R. recognized that her youngest child was not performing as well as his siblings had at that point in their educational careers. She also knew that not being recommended to the magnet school might make a temporary situation become a permanent condition. Mrs R. went to the school counselor, and then to the school liaison worker. Neither individual felt that the decision the teacher had made should be reversed. Finally, Mrs R. pleaded with the principal himself. He too said no. The list was prepared and sent to central office without her son's name on it.

Several months later, when the school personnel had likely forgotten about the conflict, the city-wide list of children selected for the magnet school was published and distributed. Mrs R's son was on the list. After her failed attempts at the school, Mrs R. had turned to her church. Through the church she had reached her local political representative. Apparently each district was entitled to a certain number of political recommendations for the special middle school, and Mrs R's son was one of them. She reported the following year that his performance in school was excellent and that he had scored in the ninety-fifth percentile in the California achievement tests. We can only speculate about what might have occurred if this youngster's tracking had not been negotiated, but certainly if he was in the process of being tracked out, his mother's actions helped him 'crash the party' to which he had not been invited. This story is noteworthy because the mother was black and on welfare — stereotypically *not* expected to do what middle-class mainstreamers do routinely.

The next example is drawn from our Alaskan data. Again a parent is in a position to negotiate for an elementary school-aged child who has been designated to the low track. Five days after John arrived in the small fishing village in southwest Alaska he was diagnosed as learning disabled. His Woodcock Johnson scores were very low, and his thinking was described as illogical. What follows is an excerpt from the research of Rodney Horikawa (1986), a UAF graduate student from Hawaii of Japanese descent. Horikawa is also a special education teacher and in that capacity documented the following events:

> *Journal Excerpt:* I dropped by Mr Robert's place at about 11:30 this morning. I had intended to stay for only a half-hour or so — just long enough to talk about John's progress and problems and ended up staying for three hours and not discussing school related matters at all. What Mr Robert and I talked about was fishing.

I'll try to reconstruct as best I can the flow of the conversation:

Mr R.: Me and John—we spend a lot of time together out in the water. The old ways are going so fast. Did your father teach you about the old way? Those things I know because I was there to see it. It was a kind of life that I just happened to meet and catch when I was a boy up there in Dillingham. These things I tell John about because he does not know them and because I caught those times.

Do you know this Hawaiian guy named Kemoe Johnson? I used to fish with this guy on Mr Pearce's boat. Man can that guy drink. He could put anyone under the table. Strong too. He could tell by looking at the water just where the fish were going to run. He told me he could hear the fish. It's strange how two natives can see fish so differently.

Say I bet you came to talk about school. You know the white man's way of studying ice is to chop a piece off and take it into his house. We natives are like ice, you take us into these schools and we're going to melt.

[*I asked him about the difference between the old ways and the white man's ways and what was the most important thing that he learned from the old ways.* Mr Roberts picked a bunch of stones. With one group he scattered them around. With the other group he made a circle of stones.]

Mr R.: The way white men fish is like this [pointing to the scattered stones]. Everything is loose and separate. The white man sees only this because he can see only this far. [He holds his hands between the two temples of his head.] It's us and them. It's the man and the fish . . . .

The old ways are like this [pointing to the circle of stones]. You tell me which is the beginning and which is the end? There's a song I learnt when I was a boy. I'll tell you in English since you can't speak our language:

> The hunter is the hunted and
> the hunted is the hunter
>
> To be full is to be hungry and
> to be hungry is to be full
>
> To be hot is to be cold and
> to be cold is to be hot.

Out on the water I try to teach John to breathe in time with the waves and to make his head open like the sea. People think too much .... Thoughts are like rocks. Too much thinking is dangerous like trying to steer your boat off Afognak (lots of rocks in the water off Afognak). These are things that I try to teach John because if he does not catch these now, he will catch something else—somebody else's ways.

John and his father left the village and the school a month later. Without a support network such as the one Mrs R. had through her church, Mr Roberts had few other options. Moving from that village was one way to control his family life and to avoid the stigma of school failure.

Mr Robert's son may have entered school in a neighboring village, but we have no data. There are no records which capture the frequent moves from city to village and back which many Alaskan native students experience. Each move is recorded as a dropout. Additionally there are some statistics to indicate that there is considerable variation in dropout rates from urban to rural settings. In the small rural villages the school is almost a community house and all the young people in the village are there all day. It makes sense to want to be there. In the cities, however, native students often experience extreme racial prejudice from their non-native peers and frequently experience low tracking and low expectations. One of my students who is half-Eskimo experienced ascription to low track classes all through her experiences at an urban high school in which she was a minority. Her only affirmation of her own intelligence came when she won the state championship for chess. She expressed a combination of bitterness and delight in surprising her high school teachers. These conditions encourage early dropout if not a move to more homogeneous rural communities if there are family ties and networks to support that.

Many rural students find themselves finishing high school in their local villages but dropping out when they get to college. In a recent paper Gilmore (1987) has detailed some of the concerns about UAF's high native attrition rates. The following example is illustrative of these undergraduates' reflections on their own experiences:

S's Voice: My elementary and high school education experience has been in a relatively small school in rural Alaska. I will return to the same school as a student teacher a few weeks from now ....

My main concern as a future Alaskan native teacher is that there is an alarming occurrence of suicide in our region. We are currently absorbing new facets of change that have permeated our society in less than a century. Many people are unable to deal directly with the new technology, large amounts of institutions and their complex bureaucracies, a cash economy. The result of this inability for transition is an extreme rate of alcoholism, child abuse, broken families, loss of cultural knowledge and a lack of confidence and self-identity in our young people.

I feel that our educational system can and must address these issues for they are realities within the community. These realities cannot be ignored because they are issues that students deal with on a daily basis.

I have experienced . . . (what Chester Pearce termed) racist 'microaggression' within my school, maybe not intentionally caused but nonetheless very real. For example, the attitude of many teachers portrayed a sense of low expectation; a sense of demeaning spirit to my own culture. Our school was almost sterile to my homelife, my community, our beliefs, values. High expectations were always there for the non-native students: many of these being the teachers' offspring.

Many students came away 'brain-washed' believing that we could never be as intelligent as the others. I may sound racist; this is not my intention as I am merely sorting out feelings that have lain submerged for a long time.

There is currently a very important need in our school system. Teachers must be able to instill within the students a sense of self-esteem and pride for being who they are. This is needed so that our youth can develop into strong individuals, so crucial for the survival through ordeals we face in our society today. Our educational system must include a cultural base process which emphasizes native world view, social roles, native professional development and research.

'S' left her student teaching experience two weeks after she began. That was one year ago. She is presently working as a secretary in a mining enterprise and is not sure whether she will return to complete her certification.

V's Voice: I grew up in a very small village and from my personal experiences I feel the teachers would come into the village with one thought on their minds, the salary is good and heck, who's going to be watching me teach. I know one thing is true, I was watching them, because I had no choice. I am saying this because the teachers who did come into the village would always stereotype us (natives), and from this would subconsciously make us feel dumb. I don't think the teachers really knew they were doing this . . . .

> When I was still in school in my village, I had a teacher tell me that 'I was going to be a dumb drunk native and never go anywhere.' I felt this way for a long time. Now I know that the teacher was very wrong. This made a lasting impression about how I felt and thought about teachers.

'V' transforms his teacher's remarks from condemning to motivating. He recalls being driven to do well in school 'just to show him he was wrong'. 'V', a junior at UAF, has 'taken the semester off'. He and his roommate are driving through the lower 48; he plans to return to school in the fall.

The final example is drawn from our Philadelphia experiences. As part of the requirements for an undergraduate course Gilmore taught in urban education at the University of Pennsylvania, Pedro Ramos collected the following interview from a second generation Puerto Rican female who was a junior at the university. She recalls an experience from her high school in the Bronx, where the dropout rate was more than 80 per cent.

Question: Describe your most powerful experience with education?
Answer: Well, when I was in tenth grade in high school, I was having a lot of problems at home and with my social life. Just in general, I was pretty much screwed up in my head and wasn't concentrating on school even though I was always pretty smart. Everybody told me that but I was just messing-up in school. First marking period we get our report cards and I had failed four classes or something like that. I hadn't failed any of the classes because I didn't understand the material but because of homework. It was pretty embarrassing obviously and my mother was upset. It was open school day and we came to school. One of the subjects I had failed was history which was a big shock because it had always been my best subject previously and even after that it was my best subject. So we came in to talk to my history teacher who was a man named Mr Green who was probably one of the best teachers I ever had. He was very dedicated and a very good teacher. He sat my mother down and he looked at me with a disgusted look on his faace and he told me,

> I don't understand why you are doing this to yourself. You are probably the smartest person in my class right now. If it weren't for you I would fall asleep in class. You're the only person that keeps the discussions going. You always have good ideas but you sabotage yourself. You're very insecure about your own ability which is ridiculous because it is obvious that you have what it takes. It is just a matter of gaining the self-confidence to put it into action. You're

Ivy League material . . . . You can go to an Ivy League school. You should be working now to try to get this . . . .

It really made a very deep impression on me. I was really shaken up because previous to that, I had always been aware of my intelligence but had never thought much of college at all, much less an Ivy League school, because in my family no one had ever been to college. My parents never assumed that I would go to college. They had . . . assumed see . . . I don't know what they assumed I would be, but they never thought of me going on after high school. He was the first person to really shock me into thinking, 'Hey, I can go on and get a college degree; not only a college degree but to go on to an Ivy League school and be one of the top in the country.' It had never occurred to me before. It really shook me up. It got me thinking a hell of a lot more about what I was doing in school and it helped me. Not that I didn't still mess around because sometimes I did, but whenever I started screwing around too much, I could always think back and remember what Mr Green had told me and say, 'Hey, don't screw it up for yourself because you do have this chance. You are smart and you have these abilities. Don't waste them!' I think that if he hadn't told me that, I might have messed up and might have not really gone on . . . . Maybe I would have ended up going to school but not a school as good as this one. He just helped me out in that way.

Mr Green similarly sent a dozen other Puerto Rican students from the same high school in the Bronx to the University of Pennsylvania. The young woman interviewed ends with the words, 'He just helped me out in that way.' What might have been an occasion to put her in a lower track, have her repeat her sophomore year, and the like, was transformed through one teacher's words which recontextualized failure into opportunity. In this school there was a dropout rate of over 90 per cent. This young woman was not part of that statistic.

Conclusion

This last vignette points to one of the important roles the school, as a social and cultural institution, can play. While the dropout problem is not simply a school problem, schools cannot be absolved from responsibility. Schooling in the United States, particularly for minority students, is predicated upon an assumption of incompetence. See, for example, Gilmore's (1982) study of shared community and school expectations of failure in west Philadelphia, Freire's (1974) banking concept of education or Wolcott's (1987) discussion of Kwakiutl schooling twenty years later. If this assumption of incompetence is the prevailing context of schooling, by the same token schools have the power to recontextualize schooling experiences.

Moll and Diaz (1987) have presented several cases where schools reorganized failure into success, and by implication demonstrate that failure itself is a fabrication (McDermott, 1987). The policy challenge of the view of dropping out developed in this essay is clear. Schools have an obligation: first, to recognize and respect the range of meanings and costs associated with staying in or leaving school; and second, to formulate policies that routinely support recontextualization and give voice to students and teachers. This will require the development of organizational frameworks that empower teachers to make decisions and to take responsible actions on their part.

References

BOPP, MICHAEL (1986) 'Culture: The Ultimate Curriculum'. Paper presented at the Bergeno Center, Dayton, Ohio, as cited in Donald Moss (1988) *Wholistic Education: A Model for Reuniting Communities and Schools.* Unpublished MEd paper. Fairbanks, AK: University of Alaska.

COLLINS, JAMES (1987) 'Using cohesion analysis to understand access to knowledge', in DAVID BLOOME (Ed.), *Literacy and Schooling*, pp. 67–97. Norwood, NJ: Ablex Publishing.

FINE, MICHELLE (1985) 'Dropping out of high school: An inside look', *Social Policy*, Fall, pp. 43–50.

FINE, MICHELLE (1986) 'Why urban adolescents drop into and out of public high school', *Teacher College Record*, **3**: pp. 393–409.

FREIRE, PAULO (1974) *Pedagogy of the Oppressed*, New York: Seabury Press.

GILMORE, PERRY (1982) 'Gimmee Room: a Cultural Approach to the Study of Attitude and Admission to Literacy'. Unpublished doctoral dissertation. University of Pennsylvania.

GILMORE, PERRY (1987) 'Sulking, stepping and tracking: The effects of attitude assessment on access to literacy', in DAVID BLOOME (Ed.), *Literacy and Schooling*, pp. 98–120. Norwood, NJ: Ablex Publishing.

GOLDMAN, SHELLY V. (1982) 'Sorting Out Sorting: How Stratification Is Managed in a Middle School'. Unpublished PhD dissertation. Columbia University.

HORIKAWA, RODNEY (1986) Unpublished Teaching Journal.

HORIKAWA, RODNEY (1987) 'Prolegomenon to Paradigm Shifts in Multi-Cultural Education: A Palimpset Based on Nataraja'. Unpublished paper prepared for Education 621; Cultural Dimensions of Language Acquisition. Fairbanks, AK: University of Alaska.

McDermott, Ray P. (1987) 'The explanation of minority failure, again', *Anthropology and Education Quarterly*, **4**: pp. 361–4.

McDermott, Ray P. and Hood, Lois (1982) 'Institutionalized psychology and the ethnography of schooling', in P. Gilmore and A. Glatthorn (Eds.), *Children In and Out of School*, pp. 232–49. Washington, DC: Center for Applied Linguistics.

Moll, Luis and Diaz, Stephen (1987) 'Change as the goal of educational research', *Anthropology and Education Quarterly*, **4**: pp. 300–11.

Ogbu, John (1987) 'Variability in minority school performance: A problem in search of explanation', *Anthropology and Education Quarterly*, **4**: pp. 312–34.

Rist, Ray C. (1970) 'Student social class and teacher expectations: The self-fulfilling prophecy in ghetto education', *Harvard Educational Review*, **3**: pp. 411–50.

Smith, David M. (1983) 'Reading and writing in the real world: Explorations in the culture of literacy', in R. P. Parker and F. A. David (Eds.), *Developing Literacy: Young Children's Use of Language*, pp. 173–89. Newark, DE: International Reading Association.

Smith, David M. (1985) 'Illiteracy as social fault', in David Bloome (Ed.), *Literacy and Schooling*, pp. 55–64. Norwood, NJ: Ablex Publishing.

Smith, David M. (1986) 'The anthropology literacy acquisition', in P. Gilmore and B. Schiefelin (Eds.), *The Acquisition of Literacy: Ethnographic Perspectives*, pp. 261–75. Norwood, NJ: Ablex Publishing.

Wolcott, Harry (1987) *Afterward: A Kwakiutl Village School 25 Years Later*, Prospect Heights, IL: Waveland Press:

Discussant's Comments:
Context and Meaning

Concha Delgado-Gaitan
University of California, Santa Barbara

Central Thoughts of Paper

Gilmore and Smith focus on themes which account for dropping out of minority school failure and illiteracy by first contextualizing the phenomena. The primary issue here is the need to 'understand' the nature and meaning of 'dropping out'. Second, the act of dropping out is far more complex than single-variable theories can explain. More specifically, the authors argue that the problem of dropping out cannot be addressed by simply tinkering with the way we do schooling. That is, contextualizing dropping out assumes that the locus of responsibility lies beyond the school level in a way that affects the school system—thus dropouts. The authors caution us against being persuaded by solutions that force the students who are labeled failures to remain in school rather than to change the system that evaluates them as failures.

In societies like the Koyukon Athabaskan children have better things to do than 'schooling'. Their native villages prepare them to survive. In the mainstream school system we do not prepare these students very well to do anything, but they are labeled failures if they do not fit in. Yet the minority students' painful socialization process into their own culture tells us that they are willing to struggle to belong if it has meaning.

General Framework

Gilmore and Smith's paper helps us to conceptualize dropouts in a much wider perspective in Alaska, where most minority students are classified as failures. The message is that *students are not failing, rather the system is failing the students.* The general assumption is that the dropout phenomenon is a construction of Western society which is non-existent in non-Western cultures. Schools in the US have linked attributes that are presumed to be indexes of failure and have ascribed them to students who do not fit the middle-class mainstream profile valued by the school, thus a dropout.

Germane to this problem of ethnocentric middle-class values is the insistence of the school to assemble into one group all possible reasons for leaving school including *involuntary* leaves like dropping out due to economic problems, pushed out by intolerant school personnel as well as the *voluntary* capricious motives for escaping, such as the political candidate Joe Biden had. Along with voluntary and involuntary motives, the temporary and permanent departures from school all appear as one monolithic explanation to the school as to why students drop out. This masks the real and complex conditions that exist. The school has been incapable of identifying non-participation in its specific context because it insists on perceiving itself as a perfect unchangeable system. The label 'dropout' is as problematic as bilingual education and special education because they obscure their meaning and intend to blame the victim, which then becomes a motivation for compensatory programs that aim to 'rectify' the student's problem. The main concern with this is that the problem is not the students'. Blaming the student or the victim has been the practice of those who believe the deficit theory. The evidence lies in the school's insistence to measure all students against one measuring device that considers Anglo middle-class mainstream values as the goal. The task becomes one of breaking down the various levels of student participation and performance in order to address each specific issue in minority schooling.

Some Reflections of the Issues

The message conveyed to many students is: 'We do not want you.' This occurs at different levels of their schooling experience. Spindler's (1987a) Beth Anne case study showed how the teacher misperceived the degree of students' social adjustment. Those misperceptions were due to the ways in which Beth represented the image of what is desirable in American middle-class culture, i.e. hard work, validity of gratification delayed for future satisfaction, validity of respectability and cleanliness, good manners and good dress as criteria for behavior. In general, Beth fit the belief system about certain symbols and behaviors as culturally defined by the teacher.

Similar findings are supported by McDermott (1987a), who has shown that the influence of the teacher's culture and the school's perceptions of children's behavior work against the student. Once again we see that school personnel and students are caught up in a cultural drama of which we need to be aware to effect change. The Spindlers have noted that the cultural ethos in urban schools is one in which children are merely by-products, not the central concern.

Studies including Fine (1986), McDermott (1987a), Philips (1983), Spindler (1987b), Trueba (1986), and Weisner, Gallimore and Jordan (1986) evidence the features of disarticulation between school and community. There is a psychological, social and academic isolation of some children. This isolation, along with the use of a curriculum perceived by children as unrelated and meaningless, contributes to increase the distance between the school and these children's home community. This is shown by the fact that the school does not prepare children to participate actively in their community, much less in the broader economic, political and social system.

Given the dichotomization of communities and schools, there are two major views to consider. One believes that the school is a penetrable system which can be changed sufficiently to accommodate minority participation. The other focuses on local community organizations and their ability to establish goals and alternatives that are purposeful educationally, politically and socially.

My own research in Colorado (Delgado-Gaitan, 1987) shows that students, their families and the employers of this working-class community define successful and failing students quite differently than did the school. Marginality occurred for some because they started out at the bottom and remained there, some because they gained less altitude on the occupational ladder than they and their parents expected. Others were marginal because they never entered the competition. Parents and students expressed their profound dissatisfaction with the content and method of instruction as being irrelevant and meaningless in their self-fulfilment. Yet, in spite of personal and educational obstacles, many Hispanic and Anglo students remained in school and did quite well.

Differential student outcomes were due to deliberate parental interventions that advocated for them and supported them emotionally when they did not have the confidence to deal with their daily conflicts. Deprivation was keenest for those who went to school and felt that they were led to believe that they had a chance to get to the top, only to find that competition eliminated them. The majority, however, were led to believe that they did not have a chance because they belonged to the Chicano working class. Mrs Cruz, a parent, illustrates this when she tells of a conference with her high school daughter's math teacher, 'I met with the teacher because I wanted to know why my daughter received a (c-) on her report card. The teacher looked at me and said that I had nothing to worry because after all that grade was pretty good for students in this community. As a parent who cares about my children's education, I don't have a choice but to continue pushing the school to deal fairly with my kids.'

On this micro-social level mentorship and different ways in which parents, teachers and other sponsors commit themselves to the realization of an 'individual's potential' expose the system for its perilous neglect of the students' total development (Levine and White, 1986).

Change must be culture-specific (Levine and White, 1986). This assumes that individuals in all societies acquire social identities based on cultural models of the life span available in the environments in which they grew up, and that these social identities include goals that motivate long-term commitments of attention and effort along certain 'pathways' (Levine and White's, 1986, term), according to a culturally organized plan or script. Anthropological evidence suggests that, in order for economic gains, prestige, power, or other culturally-defined motivating factors to exert influence on people, people must first internalize the linguistic and cultural meaning associated with such factors.

From Research to Change

The conceptual questions raised by Gilmore and Smith force us to deal with methodological issues pertaining to dropouts. The question is: how do we go about finding out what we need to know about students whom the system is failing? The approach cannot be separated from what we need to do. Methodological models must allow for active participation of students, parents and teachers in the communities we study. A research model attempted by Moll and Diaz (1987), termed 'ethnographic pedagogy', reminds us that learning is socially constructed, and if we can conceive of failure as such, then we can reorganize the activity setting for success—an effort successfully implemented by the Kamehameha KEEP. Certainly, this focus is in changing the school to accommodate minority children.

Only through these processes can change occur beyond the level that Cuban (1987) calls the 'first-order' — where single factor change occurs in the order of new textbooks, or new induction methods for teachers. 'Second-order changes', on the other hand, seek to alter the fundamental ways in which organizations are constructed due to major dissatisfaction with present arrangements. This is what Gilmore and Smith impress upon us in their stories of young Alaskan children.

While studying ways to change the school, we cannot ignore ways that the community can be empowered to discover knowledge and meaning for its own purposes. The need here is for research models to bring communities to a level of awareness of their own conditions and allow them to generate their own goals in developing educational alternatives. This calls for paradigms beyond traditional ethnography. Although describing the phenomena of cultural process through traditional ethnography, our understanding is limited to an awareness level.

Other possibilities emerge as we consider the need for teachers to become more integrally involved in remaking their own professional culture. Such potential leads us to the work of Freire (1970), whose concept of 'critical pedagogy', as applied to American society, engages people in their enculturation process. This applies to children as well as adults entering a new experience in traditional institutions. Freire's goals for critical pedagogy support the basic tenets of ethnography by considering the integrity of the specific culture. His model goes beyond mere description, however. It aims to educate people in the skills necessary so that they can de-enculturate themselves individually and collectively — thereby reasserting greater control over their lives as social and historical beings. This allows people to confront the process by which ideologies are created such as the system of interdependent beliefs, traditions and principles held by the group.

No ideal paradigm exists for conducting research for change. What is clear is that change is required from conceptualization schemes to dynamic research models. In relation to dropouts we must learn from the legacy of the 'anthropology of literacy research' which after a decade has made little impact on policy or change in the field, cross-cultural description notwithstanding. We can no longer conceive of anthropological research on academic premises without having an impact on policy and practice for the purpose of improving human potential. As Gilmore and Smith contend, the challenge for anthropologists and educators interested in dropouts lies in directing intellectual endeavors to an imperative for action.

References

CUBAN, L. (1987) 'Constancy and Change in Schools (1880's to the present)'. Paper presented at the Inaugural Conference of the Benton Center for Curriculum and Instruction, University of Chicago, May.

DELGADO-GAITAN, C. (1987) 'Compassion and concern: Mentoring students through high school', *Urban Education*, **8**, 2: pp. 93–102.

EVERHART, R. B. (1987) 'Critical Pedagogy and Teachers Education: Toward an Anthropology in Education?' Paper presented at the American Anthropological Association, Chicago, 18–22 November.

FINE, M. (1986) 'Why urban adolescents drop into and out of public high school', *Teachers College Record*, **87**, 3: pp. 393–410.

FREIRE, P. (1970) 'Conscientization: Cultural action for freedom', *Harvard Education Review*, **40**, 3: pp. 452–77.

LEVINE, R. and WHITE, M. (1986) *Human Conditions*, New York: Routledge and Kegan Paul.

MCDERMOTT, R. (1987a) 'Achieving school failure: An anthropological approach to illiteracy and social stratification', in G. SPINDLER (Ed.), *Education and Cultural Process: Anthropological Approaches*, 2nd ed., pp. 173–209. Prospect Heights, IL: Waveland Press.

MCDERMOTT, R. (1987b) 'The explanation of minority school failure, again', *Anthropology and Education Quarterly*, **18**, 4: pp. 361–4.

MOLL, L. C. and DIAZ, S. (1987) 'Change as a goal of educational research', *Anthropology and Education Quarterly*, **18**, 4: pp. 300–11.

PHILLIPS, S. (1983) *Invisible Culture*, New York: Longman.

SPINDLER, G. (1987a) Beth Anne: A case of culturally defined adjustment and teacher perceptions', in G. SPINDLER (Ed.), *Educational and Cultural Process: Anthropological Approaches*. 2nd ed., pp. 230–45. Prospect Height, IL: Waveland Press.

SPINDLER, G. (1987b) 'Why have minority groups in North America been disadvantaged by their schools', in G. SPINDLER (Ed.), *Education and Cultural Process: Anthropological Approaches.*, 2nd ed., pp. 160–73. Prospect Heights, IL: Waveland Press.

TRUEBA, H. (1986) Review of *Beyond language: Social and cultural factors in schooling language minority students*, in *Anthropology and Education Quarterly*, **17**, 4: pp. 255–9.

TRUEBA, H. (1988) 'Culturally-based Explanations of Minority Students' Academic Achievement: Caste-like Minorities?' Paper presented at the Conference on Culturally-Based Analytical Models on Dropout Phenomena, Stanford University, 26 February.

WEISNER, T., GALLIMORE, R. and JORDAN, C. (1986) 'Unpackaging Cultural Effects on Classroom Learning: Hawaiian Peer Assistance and Child-Generated Activities'. Unpublished manuscript. University of California, Los Angeles.

Chapter 5

Psychosocial Aspects of Achievement Motivation among Recent Hispanic Immigrants

Marcelo M. Suarez-Orozco
Department of Anthropology, University of California, San Diego

To Drop or Not to Drop? That Is Not the Question

From 1981 until 1984, armed with what Elizabeth Coslon calls our precious anthropological 'right to be ignorant' about a people or institution (Colson, 1974:xv), I went about trying to understand how Hispanic youngsters tried to learn in US schools. During the first project from 1981 until 1983 I was part of a large research team of University of California, Berkeley educators, sociologists, psychologists and anthropologists studying the experiences of a group of immigrant Mexican families and their youngsters bused to a suburban school near a large industrial center in the southwest. A number of publications explore issues of educational adaptation and patterns of learning and non-learning among the youngsters (Suarez-Orozco, 1986, 1987a, 1987b). I will not dwell on those findings, although this earlier study first sensitized me to the theme I wish to consider in this chapter. What became almost at once intellectually challenging was to explore why these youngsters, given their special circumstances, should stay in school and *not* why many would leave schools or experience difficulties in learning.

Rather than discussing the strengths and weaknesses, pros and cons of the various known models which had been proposed by cultural ecologists, psychological anthropologists, sociolinguists, applied ethnographers and others to explain dropout patterns from our schools, I will explore the theoretical implications of my ethnographic research among minority youths as they went about the very difficult task of trying to learn and trying to stay in inner-city schools. In this chapter I ask not why minority youths should leave schools or experience problems, but rather why they remain at all.

Models which have endeavored to explain school failure and dropout patterns within specific and object competing theoretical discourses ('cultural deprivation', 'discontinuities', 'cultural ecological adaptations', etc.) have traditionally neglected the epistemologically prior and arguably more difficult question of why minority youngsters should stay in inner-city schools. By concentrating on failure we have failed to explore the lessons derivative from this more fundamental issue.

In this chapter I explore psychosocial aspects of achievement motivation among a group of new arrivals from Central America. Given their adverse circumstances in the inner city (see below), their linguistic and cultural discontinuities from the school system, the rather poisonous inner-city school atmosphere, the pressures to work to help the family, the fact that most of them had left one or more members of their nuclear family in the midst of the Central American wars, and their prior experiences with war and scarcity (Durham, 1979; Arroyo and Eth, 1985; Suarez-Orozco, 1987c, in press), it would be expected that if not all, certainly the great majority of these youngsters would leave schools or experience serious difficulties in learning. Many new arrivals do experience difficulties and must leave schools (Suarez-Orozco, in press), yet that is not the intellectually challenging problem. The challenging question is: why would *any* of these youngsters remain in school?

In fact many of the new arrivals did remain in schools, learned the language, graduated and went on to enroll in college or professional training programs. In so doing they seem to violate the predictions of model-makers and, more importantly, give evidence of a motivational complex that is of theoretical interests to students of migration and minority adaptation to schooling. In the following pages I scrutinize in some detail their specific emerging motivational pattern. Following a necessarily brief description of the ethnographic results, I will explore the implications of these findings for a historically key theoretical model for the understanding of human motivation and achievement, namely the pioneer work in academic psychology of David McClelland and his associates. Lastly, I will relate the implications of this critique to our current thinking on minority status and schooling in plural societies.

Escape to Freedom

By the early 1980s, as the killings in Central America had reached an unparalleled crescendo, American inner cities became reluctant shelter to thousands of new arrivals principally from El Salvador, Guatemala and Nicaragua. Escaping the Central American wars and scarcity, youths have been entering the United States by the tens of thousands in the last decade (LaFeber, 1984; Mohn, 1983). In the process of resettling in this affluent society the new arrivals came to share a dream with earlier generations of migrants worldwide: to establish themselves in an advantageous position, to be able to help loved ones still living and struggling in the old country. In pursuing their dream they came to endure great sacrifices against an emerging belief that their contemporaneous hardships would in the future bring them and their loved ones the benefits of a more decent life.

As this cohort of new arrivals began to emerge slowly from the numbing terror they had left behind physically if not psychologically (close to 100,000 politically motivated killings in Guatemala in the last fifteen years, close to 50,000 political deaths in El Salvador in the last ten years, close to 50,000 political killings in Nicaragua during the war against Somoza, thousands more since the Sandinistas took over and the contras began to operate), they began to orient themselves in the inner city, trying to get jobs and, above all, trying to learn the language and earn a credential that would open for them opportunities for a better tomorrow.

I spent a year in the *barrios* among the new arrivals, following them in their very first steps in the host society. The present analysis is thus valid so far as it rests on data on their very first adaptations and beliefs regarding the host society and their place within it. As was the case with prior immigrant experiences, longitudinal changes in strategies and worldview are certainly expected as this cohort of new arrivals becomes increasingly versed in inner-city dynamics and opportunities.

I conducted extensive ethnographic interviews with some fifty core informants from El Salvador, Guatemala and Nicaragua. All of my informants had entered the United States within the five years prior to the research. Of the fifty, thirty were males aged 14 to 19 and twenty were females in the same age range. In addition, I worked in an inner-city school as 'Bilingual Community Liaison'. This position gave me regular access to classrooms, put me in daily contact with teachers, counselors, administrators, parents and relatives of most bilingual students. I also worked, *ad honorem*, in a second inner-city school with a high concentration of new arrivals. Towards the end of the ethnography I collected projective materials from my core informants, including dreams and over 400 Thematic Apperception Test Stories (TAT). These materials were eventually transcribed, translated from Spanish into English, scored and analyzed. Elsewhere (Suarez-Orozco, 1987c, 1989) I explore how the projective materials served the new arrivals as plastic media to explore emotionally laden subjects (torture, terror, guilt, shame, etc.) in a manner that was less threatening than direct questioning or repeated prodding. In their dreams and in their responses to the TAT, they spoke of the unspeakable with greater elaboration than they could upon direct questioning.

Much to my surprise all of the fifty core informants remained enrolled in schools. Other recent arrivals did leave schools but I will not tell their stories here. Suffice it to note that those who did leave schools often did so in order to devote themselves more fully to work for money to share with their less fortunate relatives back in Central America. Therefore, even among those new arrivals leaving schools a concern with nurturance (see below) over less fortunate folk was a central factor in their strategies in the new land.

As is true with the Hispanic population at large, the youngsters in my study went to predominantly minority schools which were overcrowded and understaffed (see Hispanic Policy Development Project [HPDP], 1984). The student body was in both cases over 90 per cent minority. Both institutions had extremely high mobility rates (about 700 adds and some other 700 drops from the rosters) during the academic year. The schools were located in particularly decayed neighborhoods in the inner city. Prostitutes sold their services within a three-block radius of the schools. Pushers regularly peddled their drugs all around the schools. Marijuana, hashish, cocaine, crack, barbiturates, speed and other drugs were readily available in the school yard. Street people, many with obvious psychotic problems, could be found wandering aimlessly in the vicinity.

Both schools had bad reputations in the city for gang violence. Even towards the end of the study I felt jarred by the frequent sight of city police cars and ambulances with flashing lights parked in front of the schools. An unhealthy sense of fear permeated the schools. In a perverse twist, the new arrivals, most particularly the young women in my sample, traded their old Central American terrors for new inner-city living fears. The young women lived in fear of being assaulted on the way to and from school and to and from work. The teachers in these schools were vocal about their fear of students. The new arrivals from Central America grew afraid of members of other ethnic groups. Informants routinely reported that their peers stole their bus passes. Many immigrants were beaten and robbed in the schools.

One of the schools I came to know well had a bilingual counselor (one to about 350 Spanish-speaking students). The other school had no bilingual counselor. The bilingual counselor in the one school was not a counselor by training but a teacher who, as she put it, 'had had it in the classroom', and maneuvered her way to the counseling office. The ratio of 350 students to one counselor is far from ideal, particularly taking into consideration the very special needs of a population like the one found in these schools. Their personal experience of the terrors of war, and the fact that many of them lived away from their nuclear families, posed special burdens on the new arrivals, which would conceivably make the demands on the bilingual counselor all the more acute.

Rather than addressing any such concerns, the counselors saw as their primary duty the mechanical processing of new arrivals, and with as little personal contact as possible, into 'non-academic' programs of study. 'They are not college material', a counselor told me during my work in her office. As is true with most Hispanics in the US, the new arrivals were enrolled in overcrowded, low level courses (see HPDP, 1984). Often they were pushed into courses they had already studied and completed *successfully* in their country of origin. One informant commented with some rage how the counselor had enrolled him in a low level math class he had already passed in his Guatemalan school. When he went to ask the counselor to change the course for a more challenging class, the counselor said no, because 'math in Guatemala is different from American math!'

Likewise, in her psychosocial study of five recent immigrant families from Guatemala, Vlach found an immigrant achievement involution, coupled with serious concerns over the quality of education in the inner city:

> They ['Walter family'] feel there is too much drug-taking, loose morality and not enough control of the behavior of these adolescents [in school]. They also feel that the work is too easy for Laura [one of the Walter's daughters]. She is doing extremely well and has even been moved up a grade so that she [at 12] is in classes with primarily 13 and 14 year olds. The parents feel that Guatemala is definitely superior to what they have found here (Vlach, 1984:64–5).

Perhaps the most damaging gatekeeping was done in the name of the theoretically noble idea of teaching English as a second language. The ESL program was, according to ESL teachers themselves, the school's own inner 'ghetto'. ESL courses were overcrowded and understaffed, regularly enrolling between thirty and thirty-five students per class. During the research I discovered how the Central Americans were often kept in ESL classes against their wishes and regardless of their English level because there was no room for them in the regular English program.

Teachers here felt helpless: overworked and held in low esteem, without proper materials, they felt they were expected to perform miracles in the classroom.

In summary, the new arrivals were routed into the two worst schools in the district, schools of the type that has made the American inner-city educational system infamous worldwide. Both schools were widely known for gang violence and poor academic performance. The counselors, often guided by a prejudicial agenda, tracked the new arrivals into low level, overcrowded courses, in low level overcrowded schools.

Like other Hispanics in American schools, the new arrivals were more likely to work than their non-Hispanic peers while attending school full-time (HPDP, 1984). Sixty-eight per cent of the youngsters in my sample worked while attending school; and 6 per cent worked full-time while attending schools. The majority of these youngsters worked not only for their own needs but more specifically to help their relatives left behind. Remittances were sent regularly to Central America. Estimates indicate that recent arrivals from El Salvador alone send some 400–600 million dollars annually to that troubled country (Pear, 1987). Informants commonly reported that the work routine seriously affected their schooling.

Despite these problems my core informants remained in schools, and five of the graduating seniors in this sample went on to enroll in college.

Survivor's Teleology or the Psychocultural Importance of 'Being a Somebody'

Despite a poisonous inner-city atmosphere of drugs, violence, low expectation, the calculated tracking of minority students to unacademic subjects (in already unacademic schools), bitter teachers, the seductive offers by more acculturated peers to join the street culture and the need to work to help the family, these informants remained in the inner-city institutions, trying to learn English. Considering the legacy of economic scarcity and political terror in Central America (see Suarez-Orozco, in press; Arroyo and Eth, 1985; Durham, 1979), it is remarkable that any of these youngsters should stay in the inner-city schools, trying to 'become somebody', as they would tell me.

Perhaps the overriding interpersonal issue facing the youth I worked with was that even though they had escaped, many of their loved ones remained in an eerie scenario of collective terror and scarcity. This fact created unique interpersonal concerns and intrapsychic preoccupations in this cohort of immigrant youths. The majority of my key informants continued to be affected one way or another by the uncertain fate of the less fortunate folk at home. Note that 64 per cent of the youths in my study had one or more members of their nuclear family still residing in a war-torn Central American nation. This is not counting less immediate relatives and friends left behind. Others, particularly young men, had left their entire nuclear family in Central America and were living in the US with distant relatives or friends. In most cases parents had used vital resources to send a youth to the safety of the United States.

Important psychosocial issues derive from these facts. Among these immigrants, particularly among the older and more mature youths (in the 17–19 age range), I found a severe sense of responsibility to those left behind. Survival strategies in the new land were often framed in reference to a plan to rescue those relatives still in the midst of the Central American wars (Suarez-Orozco, 1987c, in press). Among the ones lucky enough to have both parents and siblings with them in the inner city (seventeen of fifty or 34 per cent of the sample), the sense of duty to parents and folk remains strong. Often an inner sense of obligation to others is translated into concrete strategies for nurturing those who have sacrificed on their behalf. As a Salvadorean teenage put it,

> I now work and study because I want to help my parents. They sent me to this country so we could get ahead. It is very hard (*muy difícil*) [to both work and study] because English is not my first language. But I want to help them. And in the future I want to be a teacher because I like to help others. I would like to help other Latinos here get ahead in this country. Now I tutor them [other Latinos] during the lunch hour. I help them with algebra and biology. I want to be an example to them and to my brothers. I want to help.

Another informant spoke of the expressive side of becoming a somebody — 'un universitario': 'I believe the most important thing I can do for my parents is to become a Doctor, that would make them happy. I will be the first professional in my family. She [mother] does not want me to lead a life such as they had to live when they were young. They had a hard life. They had to work hard, sacrifice themselves.' More than once I heard the phrase, 'They [parents] want me to be what they could not be'. Another informant noted, 'Studying is the most important thing I can do now. Graduating [from college] will bring my parents the satisfaction that I have become somebody, I will be a professional. I will be the first professional in my family. And that is what my parents want. They could not go to school. I have a chance now to make up for their deprivations by becoming a professional.'

In these narratives achievement themes are not framed in terms of individualistic preoccupations with self-advancement or materialistic well-being, but are expressive of a wish to 'make up' for prior sacrifices and deprivations of loved ones responsible for sending them out to freedom. In this world to be 'a somebody' is to nurture loved ones; to forget loved ones and their pains is to be a nobody. Among many informants in this cohort of new arrivals something akin to 'survivor guilt' appeared (Bettelheim, 1980:274–314). The syndrome experienced by many of the recent arrivals from Central America is similar in some aspects to the guilt described by Bruno Bettelheim occurring among survivors of the Nazi death machine. Bettelheim described how many survivors in the death camps shared a belief that one's life was spared because someone else had suffered or died.

The 'guilt', that I argue is a key for understanding the motivational dynamics of this cohort of new immigrants, emerges in ongoing interpersonal concerns and intrapsychic tensions. It does not appear to be rooted in a Central American cultural syndrome or socialization pattern that would make the youngsters particularly prone to feelings of guilt. Therefore, I am not here concerned with the debate in anthropology over the socialization of 'guilt' versus 'shame' in different societies (DeVos, 1973:144–64; Obeyesekere, 1981). In the Central American context guilt patterns seem not to be the product of specific culturally constituted socialization practices. Rather feelings of guilt seem to be *emergent* in the process of change relating to the specifics of resettlement in the new land.

Any system of morality is rooted in the human capacity for awareness that action and thought have consequences on the social environment. In that sense morality, although dependent on the capacity to internalize shared values and norms in inner psychic structures, is also part of the transactional social order. Developmentally human beings become more aware of their own capacity both to 'hurt' and 'help' others by acting or by failing to act in a certain fashion (Piaget, 1930). From early childhood onwards humans begin to locate their acts, as well as failures to act, in a larger system of interpersonal causality, for an actor in a social scene to do and to fail to do is bound to have consequences for others.

In any normally adjusted person the awareness that one's behavior or condition may directly or indirectly create suffering in others makes one prone to feelings of guilt. The propensity to guilt among the new immigrants from Central America principally derives from: (1) an insight that loved ones have had to sacrifice for them to secure their well-being; (2) an awareness that they have been selected over others, often siblings, to enjoy the relative security of life in the US; and (3) an awareness of opportunities for advancement in this more affluent society not available to those left behind. Such awareness creates a propensity to intense guilt should they fail in their social duties. Should these feelings occur, they can be assuaged by expiatory re-application to the task at hand. As Bettelheim has written, to survive for many meant living with the certainty that one had survived 'for a purpose' (Bettelheim, 1980:393). The importance of being a somebody is related to the new arrival's special 'purpose': to help alleviate the continuous suffering of loved ones.

Among many new arrivals in my sample feelings of desperation give way to a harsh sense of responsibility that they must now seize upon any opportunities. Achieving in school and working to ease parental hardships are intimately related to this psychosocial syndrome of propensity to guilt over one's selective survival.

Hermes in the Barrios: A Psychocultural Critique of Motivation Theory

Next I wish to explore the specific motivational pattern I have isolated among the new arrivals in the context of the larger theoretical work on achievement motivation. I argue that among the Central American refugees the dream to 'become somebody' flourished in a very specific cluster of social perceptions and interpersonal concerns.

On the instrumental level, achievement motivation among the new immigrants was primarily associated with a desire to gain a position that would enable them to help others materially, such as relatives still in Central America. Also among many new immigrants the dream to achieve a profession could be related to a wish to make parental sacrifices worthwhile by achieving in the new land what the parents could not in Central America (Suarez-Orozco, in press).

In the next section I explore the relationship between need-achievement and the socialization of independence studied by David McClelland and his associates at Harvard in their classic studies of achievement motivation and the cluster crystallized in the Central American data. I shall defend the proposition that McClelland's achievement-independence cluster may be useful to explore a culture-bound motivational pattern, yet, contrary to McClelland's claims, the model is largely inadequate to explain the motivational dynamics manifest in immigrant Hispanics.

McClelland and his associates have been pioneers in the systematic study of human motivation (see, for example, McClelland, Atkinson, Clark and Lowell, 1953; McClelland, 1955, 1961, 1984; McClelland, Baldwin, Bronfenbrenner and Strodtbeck, 1958; Stewart, 1982).

Influenced by some basic Freudian principles, they view human motivation as related to certain affective processes. McClelland and his group concentrated their efforts in capturing achievement motivation, defined by them as the need for 'competition with a standard of excellence' (McClelland *et al.*, 1953:161) in the products of human fantasy. They attempted to document achievement themes under various experimental conditions through the use of projective tests, including the Thematic Apperception Test, and also through the study of folklore, more specifically folktales (McClelland *et al.*, 1953:97–161). They sought the foundations of achievement motivation in certain cultural and family dynamics.

> In the case of achievement motivation, the situation should involve a 'standard of excellence,' presumably imposed on the child by the culture, or more particularly by the parents as representatives of the culture, and the behavior should involve either 'competition' with those standards of excellence or attempts to meet them which, if successful, provide positive affect or, if unsuccessful, negative affect. It follows that those cultures or families which stress 'competition with standards of excellence' or which insist *that the child be able to perform certain tasks well by himself* — such cultures or families should produce children with high achievement motivation (McClelland *et al.*, 1953:275).

The next question is *precisely how and in what social contexts* is this taught? What are the specific processes significant in the training of achievement motivation? McClelland's hypothesis is that 'individuals with high achievement motivation will have been forced to master problems on their own more often and earlier than individuals with low achievement motivation' (McClelland *et al.*, 1953:276). Thus in this model achievement motivation and 'independence training' are intimately related.[1]

McClelland's group identified a number of specific variables which foster achievement motivation; for example, among American college students,

> A 'felt lack of love' is associated with high *n* Achievement. The largest single correlation involves the rejection attributed to the fathers by their sons; that is, sons who felt their fathers had rejected them had higher *n* Achievement scores than those who felt their fathers had loved them and accepted them (McClelland *et al.*, 1953:279–80).

Second, 'Sons with high *n* Achievement tend to perceive their fathers as unfriendly and unhelpful' (*ibid.*). In a sample of American college students, those who

> give evidence of being very 'close' to their parents in their admiration of them and perception of them as particularly loving and helpful do not for the most part score high on *n* Achievement. On the contrary, it is the students who see their parents as 'distant' — unfriendly, severe, unsuccessful — who have high *n* Achievement scores (*ibid.*: 281).

Subsequent studies among American high school students led McClelland and his followers to conclude that there are optimal levels of perceived parental aloofness which are associated with high achievement motivation: too much or too little perceived parental rejection may both be counter-productive to the emergence of a robust achievement motive (see also Rosen and D'Andrade, 1965:375–99).

To summarize, this model argues that achievement motivation is intimately related to a socialization pattern that puts emphasis on the training of *independence*. The more and the earlier parents pushed their children to become independent, and to turn to themselves to solve problems, the more the motivation to achieve would be fostered. High achievement motive mothers teach their would-be high achievement motive children that they are independent, and that they are on 'their own' to solve problems. Veroff found that mothers with high achievement motive were somewhat distant and saw their 'children as interfering with their use of time' (Veroff, in Stewart, 1982:114).

McClelland's model captures an unmistakably *Protestant* socialization pattern rooted in a specific ethic, embedded within a socioeconomic climate. Indeed, one of McClelland's objectives, according to LeVine (1967), was to explore how 'the protestant ethic' (Weber, 1958) was translated into concrete socialization patterns adapted to a capitalistic mode of production. According to this model, increasing industrial, technological and bureaucratic specialization would require the new workers independently and autonomously to discharge their duties. Thus socialization for achievement occurs in an atmosphere emphasizing self-reliance, individualism and the sense that one 'stands on one's own' at an early age.

Yet McClelland and associates were not content with identifying and documenting the dynamics of what is essentially an Anglo-American and north European's oicotype. Like some other psychologists, McClelland claimed that his model had a wider, indeed *universal* application to 'children in all cultures' (McClelland *et al.*, 1953:289). Here this explanatory system becomes increasingly problematic.

Marcelo M. Suarez-Orozco

Before exploring how the Central American data make questionable the proposition that achievement motivation is intimately related to a form of rugged individualism, I must first consider how McClelland explored the universalistic applications of his model. After all, they wrote: 'We do not want to develop a theory of motivation or a method of scoring for achievement motivation which will apply only to middle-class White American males. The theory as stated is more general than that and *should apply to children in all cultures*' (McClelland *et al.*, 1953:289; my emphasis).

To test the universality of the achievement/individualism model McClelland and associates turned to a thematic analysis of achievement content of folktales among eight North American Indian groups. They then related the thematic content of the tale among the different Indian groups to each group's 'independence training' (McClelland *et al.*, 1953:289–97). Their treatment of the North American Indian tales and other ethnographic materials is, as we shall presently see, far from satisfactory. First, they did not collect and analyze *multiple versions* of the folktales, as most folklorists would have advised them to do. A characteristic of folklore is the multiple existence of any given folkloristic text (Dundes, 1965:1–3; Bascom, 1965:25–33). Instead, they seemed to rely on *composite* versions of the tales. As they present the folklore data, it is impossible independently to confirm the validity of the thematic interpretations. Second, it is not clear that they were able to identify folkloristic oicotypes for specific Indian tribes. The argument would have been stronger had they been able to identify that folktale 'A', for example, a Navaho oicotype, is related to a specific cultural 'independence training pattern' *and* is not to be found among other tribes not sharing that independence training pattern. As they present their case, the possibility is not ruled out that high achievement content tale 'A' from high independence training tribe 'A' is not present in low independence training tribe 'B'. A third problem with McClelland's anthropological and folkloristic *modus operandi* is that rather than relying on their own ethnographic fieldwork to rate independence training among the various North American Indian tribes, they used as their source the ethnographically suspicious Human Relations Area Files (HRAF) which have been severely criticized on grounds of accuracy and reliability (Barnouw, 1979:145–52). In short, their own highly problematic test of the achievement-individualism cluster among eight North American Indian groups makes it plain that the cross-cultural test of the model is far from satisfactory.

Yet throughout his later writings McClelland continued to claim a cross-cultural basis for the model. For example, in his classic *The Achieving Society* (1961) he again turned to folklore, this time to capture

110

the essence of achievement motivation in Greek mythology. In the mythological figure Hermes, McClelland finds the essence of achievement motivation.

> Basically the story deals with how he [Hermes] steals the cattle of his older brother Apollo on the day he is born. He clearly has high *n* Achievement: 'It did not take long to prove his prowess to the immortal gods. Born in the morning, in the noonday he performed upon a lyre, in the evening he stole the cattle of the archer-god Apollo.' The achievement imagery is of two general types. Great stress is laid on how cunning a schemer Hermes is to outwit his powerful older brother, even though he is only a baby. 'He is litigious, skilful at making the worse appear the better reason. He lies brazenly to Apollo. He tries a mixture of trickery, bluffing, flattery, and cajoling to persuade Apollo to let him keep his cattle, and it succeeds ....' (McClelland, 1961:302).

Whether Hermes is the achievement motive archetype or a psychopathic archetype is debatable. What remains curious and revealing is that McClelland should find in such a figure the essence of achievement. McClelland believes that Hermes captures the essence of achievement motivation because he is driven by a strong desire for *independence* from his family and for self-advancement. In fact, Hermes' earliest acts include stealing cattle from his own brother and lying to his father for the sake of self-advancement.

To summarize, according to this model achievement motivation flourishes within a specific cultural climate. In this case achievement motivation is socialized within a matrix that trains youngsters to become independent from others. Indeed, high *n* Achievement subjects perceived their parents as somewhat aloof and distant. They were taught, and seemed to learn, that they are on their own and that they must face the environment by themselves as early as possible. Rather than orienting the self towards the family in order to achieve, they seem to have to turn away from the family. According to McClelland, the symbolism in Hermes' story dramatically captures a family climate in which achievement motivation grows. Little Hermes learns to achieve by not becoming paralyzed by family obligations. In fact, he early and violently turns away from his immediate family.

Conclusion

McClelland's analysis of achievement motivation would suggest that the most achievement-oriented of the recent Central American immigrants should be self-reliant individualists, 'traveling with light affective baggage',wishing to leave their parents and other folk behind in their journey through the affluent society. These youngsters should be struggling for *independence* from their parents, perhaps to gain material self-advancement to make up for being from economically 'unsuccessful' family backgrounds.

This model may correctly address achievement motivation among white middle-class Protestants, yet the achievement-individualism cluster does not fit well the subtle motivational dynamics encountered among the new immigrants from war-torn Central America. Indeed, the interpersonal concern running through the lives of the most motivated and successful of my informants was a strong wish to achieve *to be able to nurture one's parents and other less fortunate folk.* I have shown elsewhere the recurrence of an achievement-nurturance cluster in the projective imagery found in the Central American data which contrasts with McClelland's comparable Anglo-American samples. For example, the new immigrants' responses to Card Two of the TAT were almost predictable: in 50 per cent of the narratives collected the heroine achieves a career through studying in order to help end parental sacrifice. Yet McClelland's Anglo-American sample had the heroine leaving behind her 'unsuccessful' relatives, in an Hermesian quest for individualistic self-advancement (Suarez-Orozco, 1987c, in press).

The family dynamics that fostered achievement motivation among the new arrivals was almost the opposite of McClelland's model of familial ethos. Among the new arrivals perceptions of parental sacrifice were a subtle concern to be factored into the motivational patterns of the youngsters. Most youngsters were keenly aware of the continuities in a cultural chain of mutual nurturance and affiliation: many youngsters reported how their parents had had to work full-time from an early age to help their own families make ends meet in Central America. Rather than viewing their parents as aloof and distant, the new arrivals portrayed them as warm and caring: after all, they said, their parents sacrificed tremendously to settle them in the safety of the United States.

The Central American case does not fit McClelland's model of achievement motivation. The most motivated of the new immigrants from Central America were not Hermesian individualists searching for self-advancement and independence. Rather they were motivated by the dream to help others: most often less fortunate relatives remaining in war-torn Central America. The ethnographic record captured other facets of this achievement-nurturance cluster: the older, more experienced youth systematically turned to the younger or more recent arrivals to tutor them and to help them in their first steps in the new land (Suarez-Orozco, in press); and the 400–600 million dollars sent home each year by new arrivals from El Salvador point to motivation influenced concern for the well-being of those left behind.

I hope my research has pointed out some of the cross-cultural limitations of a theoretical model derived from Anglo-American research (see also DeVos, 1973:167–86). Misapplying such models to explain the issues facing 'other peoples in other places' has certain implications. For example, in the case of the Hispanic Americans it has been argued simplistically that a somehow asphyxiating cultural matrix orienting individuals heavily to the family is responsible for crippling achievement motivation. Heller (1966) has argued that Hispanic families hinder mobility and achievement in school 'by stressing . . . family ties, honor, masculinity, values that hinder mobility — and by neglecting values that are conducive to it, achievement, independence and deferred gratification' (Heller, 1966:35). Such thinking is based on an erroneous view of independence training as a sine qua non for achievement motivation.

The assumption in these narratives is that an overemphasis on 'family ties' and lack of sufficient 'independence' training somehow retard achievement motivation. A more recent article on the school dropout problem among Mexican-Americans in Texas suggests that there is 'something about the relationship of the Hispanic family to the fact that 45 per cent of Hispanic youths never graduate from high school' (LaFranchi, 1985:21); and a recent front-page article in *The New York Times* concluded that the legendary strong Hispanic family 'discourages Hispanic youths from venturing into the unfamiliar world' of education (Fiske, 1988:1–16).

The inescapable image is that family traditions of interdependence, cooperation and mutual nurturance are somehow impeding the growth of achievement motivation and the school success of children. Hispanic children, not sufficiently trained in independence patterns, remain caught in a family web of counter-productive values that hinder achievement motivation (Carter and Segura, 1979:75–122). Such reasoning typically leads to variants of an 'assimilative' genre, where cultural diversities are eventually truncated. Rodriguez's tale is one such version (Rodriguez, 1982). Achievement in his case was only possible at the expense of turning away from his family and his community. The price of his achievement was a severe sense of alienation from his group.

However, this need not be the only alternative: the permutations of the human spirit are too varied and too complex to be reduced to single encompassing formulas. In the Central American immigrant case, rather than encountering a Hermesian pattern of rugged individualism and independence, I identified the emergence of a world view that orients the self to others in the context of resettling in the new land. But the achievement concerns in these new Hispanic immigrants were not similar to those reported for the majority of Americans. Having witnessed a life-long pattern of parental deprivation, many immigrant youths wish to maximize their new opportunities, often through studying, in order to pay back parents. Informants noted how their parents had to work hard their entire lives, and even harder to move to the United States, so that they could enjoy peace and a better tomorrow. Perceptions of possible opportunities were quickly incorporated into an inner desire to bestow care upon their parents.

The Central American data strongly suggest that the kind of radical acculturation advocated by Richard Rodriguez (1982) and others as required for motivation and school success is not the only alternative. Some Central American youth, among who I worked, became very successful in the Anglo-American idiom without having to give up their ethnic identity. They did not have to turn away from their humble parents. On the contrary, their dreams and deeds were embedded in a socio-cultural matrix of family and community cooperation, affiliation and mutual nurturance.

Note

1 For a detailed consideration of the relationship between achievement and independence training see also Rosen and D'Andrade (1965:375–99). For a more recent statement on achievement motivation, also influenced by McClelland's work, see Spence (1983).

References

ARROYO, WILLIAM and ETH, SPENCER (1985) 'Children traumatized by Central American warfare', in SPENCER ETH and ROBERT S. PYNOOS (Eds.), *Post-Traumatic Stress Disorder in Children*, pp. 103–20. New York: American Psychiatric Press.
BARNOUW, VICTOR (1979) *Culture and Personality*, Homewood, IL: Dorsey Press.
BASCOM, WILLIAM R. (1965) 'Folklore and anthropology', in Alan Dundes (Ed.), *The Study of Folklore*, pp. 25–33. Englewood-Cliffs, NJ: Prentice-Hall.
BETTELHEIM, BRUNO (1980) *Surviving and Other Essays*, New York: Vintage Books.
CARTER, THOMAS P. and SEGURA, R. D. (1979) *Mexican Americans in School: A Decade of Change*, New York: College Entrance Examination.
COLSON, ELIZABETH F. (1974) 'Foreword', in JOHN U. OGBU, *The Next*

Generation: An Ethnography of Education in an Urban Neighborhood, New York: Academic Press.

DeVos, George A. (1973) *Socialization for Achievement: Essays on the Cultural Psychology of the Japanese*, Berkeley, CA: University of California Press.

Dundes, Alan (1965) 'What is folklore?', in Alan Dundes, (Ed.), *The Study of Folklore*, pp. 1–3. Englewood Cliffs, NJ: Prentice-Hall.

Durham, William (1979) *Scarcity and Survival in Central America: Ecological Origins of the Soccer War*, Stanford, CA: Stanford University Press.

Fiske, Edward, B. (1988) 'Colleges are seeking to remedy lag in their Hispanic enrollment', *The New York Times*, Sunday, 20 March, pp. 1 and 14.

Heller, Celia (1966) *Mexican-American Youth: The Forgotten Youth at the Crossroads*, New York: Random House.

Hispanic Policy Development Project (HPDP) (1984) *'Make Something Happen': Hispanics and Urban School Reform*, Vols. 1 and 2. New York: Hispanic Policy Development Project.

LaFeber, Walter (1984) *Inevitable Revolutions: The United States in Central America*, New York: W. W. Norton and Company.

LaFranchi, Howard (1985) 'Hispanic family ties are cause and cure of Hispanic dropout dilemma', *The Christian Science Monitor*, Monday, 22 April, pp. 21–2.

LeVine, Robert A. (1967) *Dreams and Deeds: Achievement Motivation in Nigeria*, Chicago, IL: University of Chicago Press.

McClelland, David C. (Ed.) (1955) *Studies in Motivation*, New York: Appleton-Century-Crofts.

McClelland, David C. (1961) *The Achieving Society*, Princeton, NJ: D. Van Nostrand.

McClelland, David C. (1984) *Motives, Personality and Society: Selected Papers*, New York: Praeger.

McClelland, David C., Atkinson, J. W., Clark, R. A. and Lowell, E. L. (1953) *The Achievement Motive*, New York: Appleton-Century-Crofts.

McClelland, David C., Baldwin, A. L., Bromfenbrenner, U. and Strodtbeck, F. L. (1958) *Talent and Society: New Perspectives in the Identification of Talent*, Princeton, NJ: D. Van Nostrand.

Mohn, Sid L. (1983) 'Central American refugees: The search for appropriate responses', *World Refugee Survey*, 25th Anniversary Issue: pp. 42–7.

Obeyesekere, Gananath (1981) *Medusa's Hair*, Chicago, IL: University of Chicago Press.

Pear, Robert (1987) 'Duarte appeals to Reagan to let Salvadoreans stay', *The New York Times*, 26 April, pp. 1–8.

Piaget, J. (1930) *The Language and Thought of the Child*, New York: Meridian.

Rodriguez, Richard (1982) *Hunger of Memory, The Education of Richard Rodriguez, An Autobiography*, Boston, MA: David R. Dodine.

Rosen, Bernard C. and D'Andrade, R. (1965) 'The psychosocial origins of achievement motivation', in Paul H. Mussen, J. J. Conger and J. Kagan (Eds.), *Readings in Child Development and Personality*, pp. 375–99. New York: Harper and Row.

Spence, Janet T. (1983) *Achievement and Achievement Motives: Psychological and Sociological Approaches*, San Francisco, CA: Freman.

Stewart, Abigail J. (Ed.) (1982) *Motivation and Society: A Volume in Honor of David C. McClelland*, San Francisco, CA: Jossey-Bass.

SUAREZ-OROZCO, MARCELO M. (1986) 'Spaanse Amerikanen: Vergelijkende Beschouwingen en Onderwijsproblemen. Tweede Generatie Immigrantenjongeren. Sociaal-culturele determinanten van hun slagen of mislukken en enkele gegevens over hun orientatie als kind en adolescent', *Culture en Migratie*, **2**: pp. 21–50.

SUAREZ-OROZCO, MARCELO M. (1987a) 'Towards a psychosocial understanding of Hispanic adaptation to American schooling', in H. TRUEBA (Ed.), *Success or Failure: Linguistic Minority Children at Home and in School*, pp. 156–68. New York, Harper and Row.

SUAREZ-OROZCO, MARCELO M. (1987b) 'Hispanic Americans: Comparative considerations and the educational problems of children', *International Migration* (Geneva), **25**, 2: pp. 141–64.

SUAREZ-OROZCO, MARCELO M. (1987c) '"Becoming Somebody": Central American immigrants in U.S. inner-city schools', *Anthropology and Education Quarterly,* **18**, 4: pp. 287–99.

SUAREZ-OROZCO, MARCELO M. (1989) *Central American Refugees and U.S. High Schools: A Psychosocial Study of Motivation and Achievement*, Stanford, CA: Stanford University Press.

VLACH, NORITA S. JONES (1984) 'America y El Alma: A study of families and adolescents who are recent United States immigrants from Guatemala', Unpublished PhD Dissertation,' University of California, San Francisco, Department of Medical Anthropology.

WEBER, MAX (1958) *The Protestant Ethic and the Spirit of Capitalism*, Trans. by Talcott Parsons. New York: Charles Scribner's Sons.

Discussant's Comments: Psychocultural Aspects of Achievement Motivation

Robert Rueda
University of Southern California

The purpose of the conference was to explore the processes that lead to academic success of student populations traditionally underrepresented in higher education. A more specific goal was to promote a 'cultural stance' (the orientation and functioning of schools as agents of cultural transmission) with respect to the school-leaving practices of certain students. Although not directly concerned with dropouts, the paper by Suarez-Orozco, in an important way, turns the question around so that the focal concern is why certain minority students remain in school in spite of the overwhelming forces which mitigate against such a course of action. More importantly, this work highlights certain theoretical as well as methodological points which are important in understanding patterns of school achievement of language minority as well as other ethnic minority students.

A Brief Historical Introduction

Although the conference focused specifically on dropouts, the phenomenon of 'dropping out' is but one indicator of academic underachievement which has its roots much earlier in the school careers of students. The more general problem is that substantial numbers of language minority and ethnic minority students are at risk for underachievement (Arias, 1986; Center for Education Statistics, 1986; Orfield, 1986), as measured not only by dropping out by test scores, grade retention, referral rates to special education, eventual educational attainment, teacher evaluations, etc. In essence, the question of dropping out has to be viewed in this larger context, as but one symptom of the larger problem of underachievement.

Even a cursory examination of the literature indicates that there is a relatively long history of work on underachievement by social and behavioral scientists. It is possible to classify much of this work into the broad categories of cultural deficit approaches and, later, cultural difference approaches.

Early explanations of academic underachievement relied heavily on supposed within-child deficits which could be pinpointed as the cause of school failure. These included, for example, deficient linguistic systems, harmful child-rearing practices, inadequate cognitive abilities, as well as other individual, family and culturally mediated factors. Yet much of the work on which these conclusions were based was characterized by narrowly prescribed methodological paradigms, and lacked ecological as well as theoretical validity. Given the concern of the conference with the contributions of anthropology to the question of underachievement, it can be argued that the anthropological perspective has been largely responsible for discounting these theoretically and methodologically unsophisticated explanatory attempts. It was largely through findings from in-context, naturalistic work by sociolinguists, educational anthropologists and others, with a focus on meaning and 'making sense' from the participant's perspective, that earlier conclusions began to be questioned. These earlier deficit-based perspectives have now largely been discounted in favor of a focus on differences between home and school-based cultural practices (Erickson, 1984; Jacob and Jordan, 1987; Jordan, 1985; Ogbu, 1982; Spindler, 1982). The work presented by Tharp (this volume), for example, represents one of the more successful attempts to increase academic achievement through culturally accommodating schooling practices (see also Moll and Diaz, 1987).

In spite of successful implementations of a 'cultural discontinuity' hypothesis as the basis for fostering academic achievement among minority students, certain problems remain. For example, there is a danger of creating cultural prototypes for various groups which then become themselves the basis for negative stereotypes. Further, the attempt to derive culturally accommodating educational practices on the basis of ethnic nomenclature can easily lead to assumptions of cultural homogeneity and undifferentiated 'culturally compatible' instruction. For example, the terms 'Hispanic' and 'Latino' (among others) are often used in discussions about the educational attainments of a number of groups including Cubans, Mexicans, South Americans, Puerto Ricans, etc. Yet one is struck by the extensive differences in the life experiences of the subjects of Suarez-Orozco's study as compared to, say, a third-generation Chicano student, or a well educated white-collar professional forced to leave Cuba for political reasons. Culture cannot be conceived as a unitary classificatory variable which has uniform effects on every member of that group. Although there is increasing awareness of these within-group differences, most often large-scale population-level data such as demographic observations are invoked to highlight differences, with relatively little attention to participant-based, subjective experiences as distinguishing factors mediating those group differences. The present study must be seen as an important contribution providing valuable insights along this dimension.

The Current Context

A more recent criticism of cultural difference explanations for school failure comes from those who have emphasized macro-level social structural variables as more important mediators of school success (Gibson, 1987; Ogbu, 1987). The 'secondary cultural discontinuity' approach (Ogbu, 1987; Jacob and Jordan, 1987) draws on differences among minority groups in academic achievement, with particular attention to the conditions under which each group has been incorporated into the United States social structure. Furthermore, this approach purposely focuses on the larger social structure (as opposed to more micro-level settings) and particular groups' adaptations to this structure.

The issues with respect to the relative importance of micro-vs. macro-level approaches are more complex than can adequately be addressed here, in any case a comprehensive discussion can be found in Jacob and Jordan (1987). However, the present work must be considered in the context of this larger debate. It is clear, for example, that larger social, political and economic forces play a key role in the adaptation of the students in Suarez-Orozco's work. Yet this work must also be considered alongside the considerable evidence of cultural differences as mediators of school achievement, and in particular the encouraging results of efforts to adapt instructional environments through the social reorganization of micro-level educational contexts. In short, both a micro- and a macro-perspective are essential in addressing questions of school failure.

Integrating Perspectives

A promising approach to integrating these perspectives has recently been advocated by Weisner, Gallimore and Jordan (1986). In essence, they propose that cultural analysis of differential achievement must have the capacity to move between data on individuals and particulars to summaries of shared patterns of behavior in the form of traits, beliefs and customs. This ability to shift between levels of analysis can be achieved if culture is conceptualized as the shaper of activity settings, or contexts for individual action, teaching and learning, and task competence. This analytical scheme permits identification of the ways in which culture specifically affects the learning of individual children, at both home and school, rather than treating it as a uniform influence mediating achievement.

To specify the mediating effects of culture on individuals, culture must be unpacked (Weisner *et al.*, 1986), which involves careful description of at least the following constituents:

> The personnel present who teach and influence children; their availability in activities throughout the child's daily routine;
> cultural scripts for conduct commonly used by participants in teaching/learning contexts that arise in natal cultural and school settings;
> the nature of tasks and activities in the daily routine, and the frequency and distribution of their performance;
> the cultural goals and motives of those present in the activity setting.

As Weisner *et al.* point out, these constituent elements represent the instantiation of cultural-level factors, and reflect evolved, adapted family responses to opportunities and constraints of the local niche. Such an analytical scheme allows one to account for the heterogeneity in achievement both between and within groups, while avoiding the dangers in assumptions of cultural homogeneity. Although the work of Suarez-Orozco is enlightening with respect to the goals and motives of the students studied, the type of framework considered here argues for a more comprehensive analysis of achievement patterns at both macro- and micro-levels.

A Contextualist/Interactional View of Cognitive Traits

Perhaps motivated by the Piagetian emphasis on the universal aspects of cognitive developmental processes, much of the work in psychology has tended to assume the invariance of the traits, processes, etc. with which it has been concerned. Such a position has led to especially erroneous conclusions in cross-cultural generalizations. In education the most common areas of misapplication of this assumed invariance have been intelligence testing and speculations about the cognitive prerequisites with which children enter the school setting. Many of the faulty conclusions derived from this work can be traced to the failure to take into account contextual variations in the display of competence as well as variations in the meaning (culturally mediated understandings) of tasks/situations used to assess them. In short, there has been a long-standing assumption that cognitive traits and abilities exist independent of the situations and tasks (activity settings) in which they are assessed. Although this idea is not new (Cole and Bruner, 1971), it has tended to be ignored in much of the psychological literature.

Fortunately, more recently a contextualist/interactionist view of development in general, and cognitive abilities in particular, has begun to be adopted (Greenfield, 1984; Rogoff and Lave, 1984; Tharp and Gallimore, 1989; Vygotsky, 1978; Wertsch, 1985a, 1985b). Much of the work carried out in this tradition has drawn heavily on the basic principles of the anthropological method. Although a complete discussion of this approach is beyond the scope of this commentary, suffice it to say that many of the deficit-oriented conclusions regarding the linguistic and/or cognitive competence of minority children have had to be revised.

Suarez-Orozco offers another example of the culturally-mediated variance of cognitive traits in his discussion of the achievement motivation model of McClelland. In fact, the original achievement motivation work suggests that the highly motivated students in the study should be relatively free of family ties and concerns and more concerned with individual independence. As the paper points out, however, his data indicate the opposite pattern. Without belaboring the point, it should be noted that lack of attention to culture as a mediating process and to the context-dependent nature of cognitive traits and abilities is problematic, especially in attempts at cross-cultural generalizations. The implications of this observation should not be lost on those investigating the variables related to academic underachievement and eventual school-leaving by minority students.

Methodological Observations

Although the previous discussion suggests the relevance of the present study in conceptualizing the dropout phenomenon, there are two exclusively methodological aspects of the present paper which deserve comment. The first concerns the use of projective methodology in the study, and the second the nature of the sample.

121

It is evident that in the study of the South American immigrants in this investigation Suarez-Orozco employed a multi-method approach over an extended period of time. This included participant observation as partially carried out as a 'community liaison', extensive interviews with some fifty core informants, and the use of projective materials including dreams and Thematic Apperception Test (TAT) stories. I would take issue with this last data collection technique, primarily on the basis of arguments raised earlier regarding the assessment of cognitive abilities and traits. Although the exact details of the scoring and analysis of the protocols are not elaborated, the use of a measure as subjective as the TAT appears to be unnecessarily inferential. Furthermore, given that translation was required, there is particular concern for the potential for error and bias. This danger is lessened through the use of triangulation of data sources and multiplicity of methods, although it is unclear to what extent the TAT data add to the more customary ethnographic techniques. In short, the data would have been just as meaningful without the more inferential TAT methodology.

With respect to the sample studied, the informants represented an interesting but perhaps not totally representative group. In essence, entire family units rarely immigrated in unison; the more common pattern was for only a select member or members of a family to leave the homeland: 64 per cent of the informants had one or more members of their nuclear family still residing in the home country. Young men, in particular, had left the entire family and were living in the US with distant relatives and/or friends. As Suarez-Orozco points out, in some cases parents had used vital resources to send a particular youth to the US for safety or economic reasons.

Given these conditions, one has to wonder how family units arrived at the decision to send a particular member to the US. For example, is it possible that the most able or brightest or motivated (with the most promise of 'making it') was selected by the family? If this were the case, the conclusions with respect to achievement motivation might need to be mediated by the nature of the selected sample of informants. In spite of these methodological points, the rather strong findings of the study provide a rich and provocative source of data for those interested in the academic achievement of minority students in the United States.

Conclusion

A major contribution of the Suarez-Orozco paper is its demonstration of the power of the ethnographic method to bring to life the everyday realities of informants. Furthermore, the intricate connections between macro-level social, political and economic forces, as well as micro-level school practices, are powerfully demonstrated. Unfortunately, it underscores the complicated differences among various minority groups, and suggests that simple solutions to the complex problem of underachievement will not be easily found.

References

ARIAS, M. B. (1986) 'The context of education for Hispanic students: An overview', *American Journal of Education*, **95**: pp. 26–57.

CENTER FOR EDUCATION STATISTICS (1986) *The Condition of Education: A Statistical Report*. Washington, DC: US Department of Education, Office of Educational Research and Improvement.

COLE, M. and BRUNER, J. (1971) 'Cultural differences and inferences about psychological processes', *American Psychol.*, **26**: p. 287.

ERICKSON, F. (1984) 'School literacy, reasoning and civility: An anthropologist's perspective', *Review of Educational Research*, **54**, 4: pp. 525–46.

GIBSON, M. (1987) 'The school performance of immigrant minorities: A comparative view', *Anthropology and Education Quarterly*, **18**, 4: pp. 262–75.

GREENFIELD, P. M. (1984) 'A theory of the teacher in the learning activities of everyday life', in B. ROGOFF and J. LAVE (Eds.), *Everyday Cognition: Its Development in Social Contexts*, pp. 117–38. Cambridge, MA: Harvard University Press.

JACOB, E. and JORDAN, C. (Eds.) (1987) 'Explaining the school performance of minority students', *Anthropology and Education Quarterly*, **18**, 4; theme issue.

JORDAN, C. (1985) 'Translating culture: From ethnographic information to educational program', *Anthropology and Education Quarterly*, **16**, 2: pp. 106–23.

MOLL, L. C. and DIAZ, S. (1987) 'Change as the goal of educational research', *Anthropology and Education Quarterly*, **18**, 4: pp. 300–11.

OGBU, J. (1982) 'Cultural discontinuities and schooling', *Anthropology and Education Quarterly*, **13**, 4: pp. 290–307.

OGBU, J. (1987) 'Variability in minority school performance: A problem in search of an explanation', *Anthropology and Education Quarterly*, **18**, 4: pp. 312–34.

ORFIELD, G. (1986) 'Hispanic education: Challenges, research, and policies', *American Journal of Education*, **95**: pp. 1–25.

ROGOFF, N. and LAVE, J. (Eds.) (1984) *Everyday Cognition: Its Development in Social Contexts*, Cambridge, MA: Harvard University Press.

SPINDLER, G. (1982) *Doing the Ethnography of Schooling: Educational Anthropology in Action*, New York: Holt, Rinehart and Winston.

THARP, R. and GALLIMORE, R. (1989) *Teaching Mind and Society: Theory and Practice of Teaching, Literacy, and Schooling*, New York: Cambridge University Press.

VYGOTSKY, L. S. (1978) *Mind in Society: The Development of Higher Psychological*

Processes, Ed. and trans. by M. COLE, V. JOHN-STEINER, S. SCRIBNER and E. SOUBERMAN. Cambridge, MA: Harvard University Press.

WEISNER, T. S., GALLIMORE, R. and JORDAN, C. (1986) 'Unpackaging Cultural Effects on Classroom Learning: Hawaiian Peer Assistance and Child-generated Activity'. Unpublished paper.

WERTSCH, J. V. (1985a) *Culture, Communication, and Cognition: Vygotskian Perspectives,* New York: Cambridge University Press.

WERTSCH, J. V. (1985b) *Vygotsky and the Social Formation and Mind,* Cambridge, MA: Harvard University Press.

WHITING, B. B. (1976) 'Unpackaging variables', in K. F. RIEGEL and J. A. MEACHAM (Eds.), *The Changing Individual in a Changing World,* pp. 303–9. Chicago, IL: Aldine.

Chapter 6

Panel Discussion and Concluding Remarks

Moderator: Larry Cuban, School of Education, Stanford University

Participants: Margaret Gibson, Louise Spindler, Leonard Valverde, Raymond McDermott, Ronald Gallimore, Robert Rueda, Concha Delgado-Gaitan, David Fetterman and members of the audience

Larry Cuban, Moderator: We have invited Margaret Gibson and Leonard Valverde to present extended comments since they did not present papers or act as discussants. Louise Spindler will comment on Margaret Gibson's paper. After their presentations we will hear from each of the other members of the panel. Their comments will be followed by an open discussion in which we hope everyone will feel free to participate.

School Persistence versus Dropping Out: A Comparative Perspective

Margaret A. Gibson, Survey Research Center, University of California, Berkeley

I'd like to focus my remarks on four issues, each of them pertinent to our discussion of minority dropout problems: first, the disparity that exists between the school performance and persistence of immigrant and non-immigrant minority students; second, the wide variations in performance that exist within a single minority group; third, the need for greater attention to the interplay among gender, class and ethnicity and the interactive influence of these identities on the school adaptation patterns of minority youth; and fourth, the need for minority youngsters to feel that they can retain their separate identities and cultures, if they so choose, and at the same time be successful in school.

Immigrant vs Non-Immigrant

There is increasing evidence in the United States and abroad that children of immigrants persist in school longer and have stronger overall academic records than non-immigrant youths, majority as well as minority, of similar class background. For example, Australian research indicates that Greek, Yugoslav and Italian children of working-class backgrounds are more likely to complete high school than white Australian students of similar class status, even when the immigrant children enter school weak in English and continue to suffer an English-language handicap throughout their school years (Clifton, Williams and Clancy, 1987; Majoribanks, 1980; Taft and Cahill, 1981). Canadian studies reveal similar patterns, with the children of non-English-speaking immigrants overrepresented in college preparatory classes (Anisef, 1975; Cummins, 1984). The academic record for students of African, Greek, Indian and Pakistani origin settled in Britain is much the same. Within each of these groups young people in their fifth year of secondary school perform better on external examinations than white, majority-group classmates (ILEA, 1987).

Similar patterns of school success exist among *immigrant minorities* in the United States.[1] As indicated in Table 1, Chinese, Japanese, Korean, Asian Indian, Vietnamese, Cuban and Filipino students all persist in school longer than non-Hispanic white youths. White youths, on the other hand, persist in school longer than black Americans, Hawaiians, Puerto Ricans, Mexican Americans and American Indians. Except for

Table 1. School Persistence by Age, Race and Spanish Origin: Percentage Enrolled in School in the United States, 1980

	18–19	20–21	22–24	25–34
		Years Old		
Chinese	83.9	74.0	50.7	21.9
Japanese	77.0	61.6	38.9	14.6
Korean	77.7	54.8	30.5	13.2
Asian Indian	72.0	54.3	39.2	14.8
Vietnamese	66.6	47.5	37.8	22.4
Cuban	65.1	44.8	28.5	12.7
Filipino	62.7	38.3	20.2	9.6
*White	53.1	33.6	17.4	8.5
Black	51.7	28.4	15.9	9.6
Hawaiian	42.2	21.7	13.5	7.3
Puerto Rican	41.8	21.7	13.1	8.0
Mexican	39.2	18.9	11.6	7.2
American Indian	38.2	19.3	12.7	8.8

Source: US Bureau of the Census (1983), Tables 123, 160 and 166.
Note: *White, non-Spanish origin.

the Mexican Americans, all the minority groups with low school persistence levels are what may be termed *involuntary* or *non-immigrant minorities*.[2]

Quantitative data of the sort provided in Table 1 must be interpreted with care since many of the more recently arrived immigrants, as well as those now well established in this country, are highly educated, affluent professionals. It is hardly surprising that their children do well in school. Small-scale descriptive studies of immigrant youths and their families make clear, however, that the pattern of immigrant school persistence pertains not only to those of privileged background, but also to those whose parents are poor, have little or no formal education, who speak little or no English, and who must cope not only with sharp conflicts between home and school cultures, but also with inferior educational programs and with the racist attitudes of majority-group peers and teachers (Blakely, 1983; Gibson, 1983, 1988; Ogbu and Matute-Bianchi, 1986; Suarez-Orozco, 1988; Sung, 1979).

The international and comparative literature indicates quite clearly that immigrant parents have higher expectations for their children's success in school than non-immigrant parents of similar class background. It indicates as well that parents' expectations and aspirations are more important to school persistence than socioeconomic status, IQ or students' actual performance in school. Immigrant parents place greater importance on conformity to school rules and on hard work than on a child's native ability. Immigrant youths, moreover, are less likely than non-immigrants to relinquish their goals of a college education even when they experience academic difficulties, or are confronted with conflict between home values and those supported by the school. Sheer persistence and hard work, in the immigrant view, are the crucial ingredients to school success.

In describing this pattern of immigrant school persistence I do not mean to suggest that all immigrant youths do well in school. There are clear variations within and among immigrant groups, and some immigrant groups exhibit few of the characteristics I have depicted as an immigrant school adaptation pattern (see also Gibson, 1988:167–83). The pattern, however, is sufficiently strong to merit our attention.

Within-Group Differences in School Persistence

In seeking to understand why some minority students are much more at risk of dropping out of school than others we need to explore not only the variations in school performance that exist among different minorities, but also variations that exist within a particular minority group and the reasons that some students within the group encounter far more difficulty in school than others. I shall focus on the school performance of Mexican-origin students, both immigrant and non-immigrant, drawing on the findings of three recently published case studies.

The first is Sylvia Valverde's (1987) comparative study of 104 Hispanic, primarily Mexican American, secondary students all from a low-income neighborhood in a southwestern city. Half were dropouts, half high school graduates. In both groups approximately 90 per cent of the parents had only an elementary education or less. More than a third of the parents in both groups were unemployed, the others for the most part having jobs as manual workers. What Valverde found was that more of the dropouts than graduates spoke English as their first language, or were classified as fluent-English proficient. A higher percentage of the graduates were immigrants from Mexico, while more of the dropouts were native born. In other words, the immigrants persisted in school in spite of their language handicap. Based on her interviews with the students, Valverde concluded that peer groups played a primary role in shaping the differing school adaptation patterns.

In the second study, a comparison of undocumented immigrant *Mexicanos* and native-born Mexican Americans, Harriet Romo (1984) found sharp differences in the way families perceived the school experiences of their children. The *Mexicano* parents, like many other immigrants, had generally positive attitudes toward the US school system. The immigrant parents also believed, by and large, that an American education and proficiency in English would provide the avenue to a better life for their children than they themselves enjoyed. The second-generation United States-born *Chicano* parents, on the other hand, Romo described as having 'acquired heightened sensitivity to subordination and discrimination' which, in turn, had resulted in alienation from the schools and skepticism about school encounters. Both sets of parents were unskilled workers, although the *Chicano* parents in Romo's study had some secondary education and spoke both English and Spanish, while the immigrant *Mexicanos* spoke only Spanish and were usually illiterate.

The third study is that of Maria Matute-Bianchi (1986), who found similar disparities in both perceptions and performance between Mexican immigrants and native-born students. Equally if not more important, Matute-Bianchi documented sharp differences within the native-born group itself relating to perceptions of discrimination. Native-born students who identified themselves as Mexican Americans, along with those who were Mexican-born, tended to do better in school than those who identified themselves as *Chicanos* and *Cholos*. The latter two groups were more likely to perceive a high degree of discrimination against Mexican Americans and more likely to feel alienated from mainstream American society than either the immigrant *Mexicanos* or those who identified themselves as Mexican Americans.

Matute-Bianchi found, moreover, that students who felt alienated from school and from mainstream society tended to make fun of their peers who were good students and who accepted school rules. In Chicano parlance such students were 'Wannabees', a Chicano term meaning 'wants to be white' or 'wants to be Anglo' (p. 204), a point I'll return to presently. Matute-Bianchi also found that substantially more of the top performing students were girls than boys, which brings me to my third issue, that of gender differences.

Gender, Class and Ethnicity

There are both quantitative and qualitative data to show that students' performance in school, including their decision to persist in school through the secondary or tertiary levels, is influenced by the interaction of gender, social class and ethnic identities. Schools need to be cognizant of the joint impact of these identities if they are to meet the needs of those students most at risk of dropping out.

In my own research in St Croix, the largest of the islands that make up the United States Virgin Islands, I found that nearly 80 per cent of the native-born Crucian boys dropped out of the public school system by age 16. On the other hand, only about 20 to 25 per cent of their sisters had left school at this point. The boys equated school authority with the persistence of slavery and the domination of poor blacks by native élites and white Americans. The girls, and interestingly, immigrant West Indian males, also black and lower-class, were less impeded in school by an oppositional identity and culture (Gibson, 1982, 1983, forthcoming).

Other studies point to a similar disparity in the school performance and persistence of black males and females in Jamaica (Williams, 1973; Foner, 1973), in the United States (Barro and Kolstad, 1987; Hess and Lauber, 1985; Hirschorn, 1988) and in Britain (Taylor, 1983:220–1; Tomlinson, 1983:41). Among some other ethnic groups, such as Bangladeshi and Arab students in Britain, the situation is reversed. In both of these cases males are far more likely than females to persist in school through the secondary level (ILEA, 1987).

All too often race, class, gender and ethnicity are examined separately. Yet by lumping all blacks together, for example, or all females, or all lower-class students, we tend to overlook significant distinctions in school performance and persistence that relate to the interaction among these several identities.

Additive and Subtractive Forms of Acculturation

All minority students in this country, immigrant and non-immigrant alike, encounter strong pressure in school to conform to the ways of the mainstream majority. Schools today, as in the past, convey to minority youngsters that to be successful in school and to be 'true Americans' they must give up their minority identities. It is no wonder that some of the Chicano youngsters in Matute-Bianchi's study viewed their more academically successful peers as 'Wannabees'. The schools themselves preach a strong message of cultural assimilation.

Signithia Fordham's research among black Americans in Washington, DC reveals a comparable response to assimilationist pressures. To be successful in school in the view of those who are doing poorly is to 'act white' (Fordham, 1988; Fordham and Ogbu, 1987). Similar findings emerge from research on West Indians in Britain and from my own work in St Croix. Many West Indian males believe that in order to survive they must resist white authority (Mullard, 1982). On the other hand, boys who do well in school feel they must disassociate themselves from their black identity and from peers in the lower tracks (Troyna, 1978). As Mary Fuller's work and my own suggest, however, different patterns exist among West Indian girls. In Britain, as in St Croix, the girls are far less likely to equate school success with acting white or forsaking their black identity (Fuller, 1980; Gibson, 1982, forthcoming).

The point I wish to emphasize is not the gender difference, although it merits more attention, but the perception on the part of many minority children that school learning is associated with acculturation and, in turn, that acquisition of cultural competencies in the ways of the majority group means, ultimately, the loss of their distinctive ethnic and cultural identities. Hence, to maintain their identity many minority youngsters believe that they must resist school authority.

Cummins (1981) calls this process 'bicultural ambivalence'. Other researchers have noted that minority beliefs about the majority culture and the role of the public schools can interfere with student achievement. Referring to indigenous minorities, such as Hawaiians and Navajos, Jordan asks: 'Is the process of becoming educated necessarily the process of becoming assimilated? If so, a very terrible choice is involved' (Jordan, Tharp and Vogt, 1986:1–2). Similarly, Kramer (1983) observes that Ute Indian students learn from their parents to view school as the 'enemy' because it fosters assimilation into the majority culture and contributes to a rejection of tribal society and traditions.

By way of contrast, at least some of the minority students who do well in school, both immigrant and non-immigrant, pursue a strategy that I have labelled *acculturation without assimilation* (Gibson, 1988). They see acquisition of skills in the majority-group language and culture in an *additive* rather than a *subtractive* fashion, leading not to a rejection of their minority-group identity but to successful participation in both mainstream and minority worlds.[3] Such a strategy for minority school success has immediate and direct implications for teacher training, curriculum development and the counseling of minority students. Rather than insisting, albeit often unconsciously, that cultural assimilation is the quid pro quo for school success, educators need to foster learning environments where students are given full opportunity to participate in the mainstream of American society while also, if they so choose, maintaining their separate identities and cultures.

Notes

1 By 'immigrant minorities' I mean groups that have voluntarily left their own country, have settled legally in a new country and enjoy the possibility of remaining there permanently. Immigrant minority in my usage refers not only to the first generation—those who are actual immigrants—but also to a group whose ancestors settled by choice in the host country and which continues to maintain a separate minority-group identity. The situations of refugees,

guest workers and undocumented workers differ significantly from those of voluntary immigrants and the degree to which their adaptation patterns are similar merits further comparative analysis.

2 Following Ogbu (1987), I use the term 'involuntary minority' to refer to those groups that have been incorporated into a society by colonization, conquest, annexation or slavery. 'Non-immigrant minority' in my usage refers not simply to those who are native-born, but to those groups that have been incorporated into the host society involuntarily.

3 I draw here from Lambert's distinction between additive and subtractive forms of bilingualism (1975:67).

References

ANISEF, PAUL (1975) 'Consequences of ethnicity for educational plans among grade 12 students', in AARON WOLFGANG (Ed.), *Education of Immigrant Students*, pp. 122–36. Toronto: Ontario Institute for Studies in Education.

BARRO, STEPHEN M. and KOLSTAD, ANDRES (1987) *Who Drops Out of High School? Findings from High School and Beyond*, Contractor Report. ERIC: ED 284 134.

BLAKELY, MARY M. (1983) 'Southeast Asian refugee parents: An inquiry into home-school communication and understanding', *Anthropology and Education Quarterly*, **14**, 1: pp. 43–68.

CLIFTON, RODNEY A., WILLIAMS, TREVOR H. and CLANCY, JEFF (1987) 'Ethnic differences in the academic attainment process in Australia', *Ethnic and Racial Studies*, **10**, 2: pp. 224–44.

CUMMINS, JAMES (1981) 'The Role of Primary Language Development in Promoting Educational Success for Language Minority Students', in *School and Language Minority Students: A Theoretical Framework*, pp. 3–49. Sacramento, CA: California State Department of Education, Office of Bilingual, Bicultural Education.

CUMMINS, JAMES (1984) *Bilingualism and Special Education*, Clevedon, Avon: Multilingual Matters.

FONER, NANCY (1973) *Status and Power in Rural Jamaica: A Study of Educational and Political Change*, New York: Teachers College Press.

FORDHAM, SIGNITHIA (1988) 'Racelessness as a factor in black students' school success: Pragmatic strategy or pyrrhic victory?' *Harvard Educational Review* (in press).

FORDHAM, SIGNITHIA and OGBU, JOHN U. (1987) 'Black students' school success: Coping with the "Burden of Acting White"', *Urban Review*, **18**, 3: pp. 1–31.

FULLER, MARY (1980) 'Black girls in a London comprehensive school', in R. DEEM (Ed.), *Schooling for Women's Work*, pp. 52–65. London: Routledge and Kegan Paul.

GIBSON, MARGARET A. (1982) 'Reputation and respectability: How competing cultural systems affect students' performance in school', *Anthropology and Education Quarterly*, **13**, 1: pp. 3–27.

GIBSON, MARGARET A. (1983) 'Ethnicity and schooling: West Indian immigrants in the United States Virgin Islands', *Ethnic Groups*, **5**, 3: pp. 173–98.

GIBSON, MARGARET A. (1988) *Accommodation without Assimilation: Sikh Immigrants in an American High School*, Ithaca, NY: Cornell University Press.

GIBSON, MARGARET A. (forthcoming) 'Race, gender, and social class: The school adaptation patterns of West Indian youths', in M. A. GIBSON and J. U. OGBU (Eds.), *Minority Status and Schooling: Immigrant vs. Nonimmigrant.*

HESS, G. ALFRED, JR. and LAUBER, DIANA (1985) *Dropouts from the Chicago Public Schools: An Analysis of the Classes of 1982, 1983, 1984*, Research Report, Chicago Panel on Public School Finances, Chicago, IL.

HIRSCHORN, MICHAEL W. (1988) 'Doctorates earned by blacks decline 26.5. Pct. in decade', *Chronicle of Higher Education*, 3 February, pp. Al, A32–3.

INNER LONDON EDUCATION AUTHORITY (ILEA) (1987) *Ethnic Background and Examination Results: 1985 and 1986*, Report P 7078, prepared by ILEA Research and Statistics, 1 July, London.

JORDAN, CATHIE, THARP, ROLAND G. and VOGT, LYNN (1986) *Differing Domains: Is Truly Bicultural Education Possible?* Working Paper, Honolulu: Kamehameha Center for Development of Early Education.

KRAMER, BETTY JO (1983) 'The dismal record continues: The Ute Indian tribe and the school system', *Ethnic Groups*, **5**, 3: pp. 151–71.

LAMBERT, WALLACE E. (1975) 'Culture and language as factors in learning and education', in AARON WOLFGANG (Ed.), *Education of Immigrant Students*, pp. 55–83. Toronto: Ontario Institute for Studies in Education.

MAJORIBANKS, KEVIN (1980) *Ethnic Families and Children's Achievements*, Sydney: George Allen and Unwin.

MATUTE-BIANCHI, MARIA EUGENIA (1986) 'Ethnic identities and patterns of school success and failure among Mexican-descent and Japanese-American students in a California high school', *American Journal of Education*, **95**, 1: pp. 235–55.

MULLARD, CHRIS (1982) 'Multiracial education in Britain: From assimilation to cultural pluralism', in JOHN TIERNEY (Ed.), *Race, Migration and Schooling*, pp. 120–33. London: Holt, Rinehart and Winston.

OGBU, JOHN U. (1987) 'Variability in minority school performance: A problem in search of an explanation', *Anthropology and Education Quarterly*, **18**, 4: pp. 312–34.

OGBU, JOHN, U. and MATUTE-BIANCHI, Maria Eugenia (1986) 'Understanding sociocultural factors: Knowledge, identity, and school adjustment', in *Beyond Language: Social and Cultural Factors in Schooling Language Minority Students*, pp. 73–142. Sacramento, CA: California State Department of Education, Office of Bilingual Education.

ROMO, HARRIET (1984) 'The Mexican origin population's differing perceptions of their children's schooling', *Social Science Quarterly*, **65**: pp. 635–50.

SUAREZ-OROZCO, MARCELO M. (1988) *In Pursuit of a Dream: The Experience of Central Americans Recently Arrived in the US*, Stanford, CA: Stanford University Press.

SUNG, BETTY LEE (1979) *Transplanted Chinese Children*. Report to the Administration for Children, Youth and Family, Department of Health, Education and Welfare, Washington, DC.

TAFT, RONALD and CAHILL, DESMOND (1981) 'Education of immigrants in Australia', in JOTI BHATNAGAR (Ed.), *Educating Immigrants*, pp. 16–46. New York: St Martin's Press.

Moderator, Larry Cuban

TAYLOR, MONICA (1983) *Caught Between: A Review of Research into the Education of Pupils of West Indian Origin*, Windsor: NFER–Nelson (first published 1981).

TOMLINSON, SALLY (1983) *Ethnic Minorities in British Schools*, London: Heinemann.

TROYNA, BARRY (1978) 'Differential commitment to ethnic identity by black youths in Britain', *New Community*, **7**, 3: pp. 406–14.

UNITED STATES BUREAU OF THE CENSUS (1983) *1980 Census of Population. Vol. 1: Characteristics of the Population*, Chap. C: General Social and Economic Characteristics, Pt. 1: US Summary, PC-80-1-C1. Washington, DC.

VALVERDE, SYLVIA A. (1987) 'A comparative study of Hispanic high school, dropouts and graduates: Why do some leave school early and some finish?' *Education and Urban Society*, **19**, 3: pp. 320–9.

WILLIAMS, ERIC (1973) 'Education in the British West Indies', in D. LOWENTHAL and L. COMITAS (Eds.), *Consequences of Class and Color*, Garden City, NY: Anchor Books.

A Comment: Gender Differences Neglected

Louise Spindler, School of Education and Department of Anthropology, Stanford University

Little attention was given in the dropout conference to females and male/female differences in adaptation to schooling or with respect to the dropout phenomenon. In all of the indepth studies that George and I have done of males and females in four changing cultures (The Menominee of Wisconsin, The Blood of Alberta, the Mistassini Cree, and in Germany) the differences in adaptation expressed in the behavior and perceptions of males and females have consistently been more significant than any relationships between adaptation and education, religion or economic status. We have made a point of collecting equal samples of responses from males and females in all of our work. The differences between them often came as a surprise, for we thought that these other factors would be more determinant. Attention to these differences have led us to examine more closely the roles that women play in the infrastructure of cultural systems. The meaning of female power and influence is often so implicit and private that its meaning is obscured. We have also found that males and females appear to perceive the choices open to them rather differently and that females more often than not opt for choices that are not available in the status quo, in contrast to males, who seem to find their lot, whatever it is, more acceptable. We would expect to find that female students would more often see education as a way out and that therefore they would be less subject to 'dropoutism'.

Margaret Gibson, in her comments at the conference, pointed to some important findings concerning females and dropping out, and spoke of the need for greater attention to the interplay among gender, class, and ethnicity. She noted a disparity in dropout rates between black males and females among teenagers in St. Crox (Virgin Islands), Britain, and the United States. As she explained it, boys tend to equate school with authority and slavery while girls felt less oppositional tendencies. This is a useful observation but we need to know why. Who influenced their modeling behavior — mothers, school teachers, the media? And why did it affect them differently than it affected the boys? Dr. Gibson also noted that the girls viewed the acquisition of skills as 'additive' rather than 'subtractive'. Again, what deeper difference in adaptation helps to explain this phenomenon.

Our studies show that females are not as committed to current roles and values, particularly in situations where they may be disadvantaged by overt male dominance, as males are to those available to them. Females are therefore more open to alternatives and certainly may see further schooling and the acquisition of marketable skills as desirable.

Whatever the reasons for male/female differences in adaptation to schooling or whatever, it is important, for our further and better understanding, to interweave gender differences with those of class and ethnicity.

Anthropology and School Dropouts: An Educator's Perspective

Leonard A. Valverde, University of Texas, San Antonio

Before the substantive discussion let me make several procedural comments. First, my focus in discussing school dropouts will be on the ethnic and racial minorities who are enrolled in public schools today and who are leaving these schools in much greater numbers than the white population. Recent surveys have revealed the high dropout trend for minorities across the country. In Texas, for example, a recent state-wide survey found that the average state dropout rate for Mexican-Americans was between 45 and 55 per cent, and in some school districts as high as 70 per cent. Also blacks exceeded white students in number of dropouts. Second, I will attempt to provide a different, but convergent set of views on the issue of dropouts, drawing on anthropology, psychology, organizational theory, sociology and economics. Third, let me make explicit one of my assumptions: that parents of minority youngsters are no different from parents of any youngsters in one aspect—they want the best for their children. In the view of most parents education is the road to success. However, there is a slight difference in the attitude of minority parents. They see schools as places where individuals acquire learning, whereas educators emphasize the socialization of minorities in schools. A final assumption is that minority children want to learn as much as other students.

Let me begin by using an anthropological construct called 'rites of passage'. George and Louise Spindler have discussed the initiation of youth into adult cultures. The initiates wanted to transform themselves from youths to adults, and to do so they needed to adopt the values, attitudes and customs of that culture. The quicker the initiate adopts the customs and values of the adults, the sooner the transformation. If we apply this construct of transformation, where initiates go through certain 'rites of passage', to students in public schools in the United States, the same outcome can be expected. However, when 'rites of passage' are applied to minorities in public schools, there is a different outcome. When schools emphasize the socialization of youngsters, particularly minority students, exclusion instead of inclusion results. The socialization of minority youngsters by means of acculturation, i.e., instilling in them the predominant societal values, becomes a transformation that they resist. That is, they and their parents do not want themselves to be made over. They do not want to lose their identity; they simply want to gain academic skills. In having to change from one cultural identity to another, minority students have to reject their identity, to question the value of their heritage and their family customs. They are, in short, being asked to adopt a new personality. What typically happens in these situations is that they either resist this transformation or leave the environment called schools, therefore, dropping out.

From an organizational point of view one can build another case for students leaving. Schools have been reported as being 'sorting machines' — institutions designed for granting social status. One way that schools sort students is through labeling, grouping and tracking procedures. Students are labeled as gifted, as disadvantaged, as mentally retarded, etc., and are thus permanently identified. It is rare that a student sheds the label of disadvantaged and then participates in regular instruction, or that a student identified as gifted and talented is reclassified into another category. While there is value in identifying youngsters for practical instructional/learning purposes, what has happened is that educators have turned this labeling, grouping and tracking set of procedures into a set formula and into a permanent status, and schools are allowing structure to dictate purpose. Lastly, school personnel are more concerned with discipline and conformity than with building students' capacity to think and develop their skills. The drive for conformity is coming close to one for uniformity. Thus, while schools concern themselves with conformity, discipline and uniformity, youngsters, particularly minorities who are diverse and different and want to maintain their individual as well as group identity, are confronted with opposing forces. Students are forced to decide whether they want to maintain status in the school; if they do, they must shed their personal identity, or if they want to keep their family and cultural identity, then they are prone to leave the school. Again, from an organizational point of view students of minority status are forced to leave.

Let me share with you a research study that was done some time ago by the sociologist, Amitai Etzioni (1961). He examined agencies to understand their organizational constructs as well as to make some comparisons and contrasts. Etzioni examined hospitals, schools, prisons, military camps and corporations. He discovered that schools resembled prisons and military institutions more than the other types of institution. While he did not make the following specific comparisons, let me share with you what I think are the similarities between schools and prisons. Principals can be seen as wardens, that is, they have the same functions — set the rules; teachers as guards — keep order; classrooms as cells; the rights of students are few and limited, as are the rights of prisoners. Furthermore, persons who come to minority schools must check in at the principal's office, much like visitors at a prison must check in to see prisoners. Prisoners in penal institutions develop their own social structure: some prisoners have high status, others no status; some gangs are powerful and others are weak. So it is with students in schools: they develop their own status—immigrants are lower in status than students who were born here. Students who are academically more able to have a higher status than others.

However, prisons are not healthy environments. Their purpose is to rehabilitate prisoners, but we all know that this rarely occurs. Schools are for the purpose of educating youngsters, but we have seen that socialization may be the more prominent purpose. The bottom line is that prisoners want to leave the institution as quickly as possible and even try to escape. Students also want to leave schools as quickly as possible and may do so illegally. This is called dropping out.

Students leaving school early can also be seen from an economic viewpoint. The two concepts labor intensive and time intensive can be applied to school dropouts. That is, teachers are hard pressed to accomplish their tasks because of limited time, more curriculum objectives, reporting and non-classroom demands such as lunch duty, playground duty, before and after school duties, committee assignments, etc. The outcome is that teachers are worn down and their capacity for quality human interaction deteriorates. Thus they are forced not to look at students on an individual or personal basis, but simply on a group basis. They are more concerned with getting through the textbook or the identified objectives than they are with the growth, development and emotional stability of youngsters. The consequences of the overdemanding tasks and insufficient time and resources are that teachers give the impression that they do not care about students, and thus students leave school. It is significant that the single most important reason given by school dropouts for leaving school is the lack of caring on the part of teachers.

I have considered, from multiple perspectives, why minority youngsters leave public schools before successfully graduating from high school. I have tried to demonstrate that it is not the fault of the youngsters or their parents. Instead the forces which promote leaving school can be found in schools, in their organization, in their purpose, in their function and in the economics of the situation. In short, leaving school for minorities is a phenomenon of cultural conflict, value transformation, lack of teacher caring and low expectations of their abilities.

Reference

ETZIONI, AMITAI (1961) *A Comparative Analysis of Complex Organizations.* Glencoe, IL: Free Press.

Panel Discussion

Larry Cuban, Moderator: Thank you Margaret Gibson, Louise Spindler and Leonard Valverde. Now if each of the remaining panelists will give their reactions to the conference papers and discussions as a whole . . . .

Raymond McDermott: 'I can't help thinking that I'm at a conference on learning disabilities twenty years ago. The great problem is that if we want to talk about dropouts, there is a language available for us, a language for naming all kinds of dropouts in the country and making believe that they are real entities, a language for assuming that we know what goes on inside their heads or how they feel about upward mobility or don't feel about upward mobility. I think we're in a great deal of trouble talking about dropouts, just as we were twenty years ago in talking about learning disabilities. That is, we don't have any idea how this stuff works in the world. How are we going to get around this?

That's the great struggle in the study of education. Where are we going to get analytic categories? How can we freeze behavioral items, freeze persons as if they were real analytic categories? . . . All those words are a part of the lexicon, part of the system that's producing the problem so those words have to be part of the problem as well, and can't survive as analytic categories. Study after study comes along and makes believe that we can identify this group and that group and that if we ask them a couple of questions we'll figure out what they really want. When in fact it seems to me that the people out there, their words are always eloquent, always interesting, if you get the right angle on them. But if you just show up and say, 'what do you think?', 'what do you know?', 'what do you want?', they can't tell you any more than you can tell yourself.

I think that what happened in the learning disabilities field for a long time is that we kept coming up with enough anomalous findings so that we could fight our way out so we could come up with a new sense of learning disabilities. My definition of a learning disability . . . is that in schools there is a place for learning disabilities before you ever show up. And what learning disabilities are behaviourally is that you spend your time arranging to not get caught not knowing something. And there's always somebody to catch you. There's always some new test, some file to put you in, and you might get caught.

Ronald Gallimore: We can spend a lot of time analyzing dropouts and other school-related problems, but there is one thing that's got to happen as an institutional change. There has to be an intermediate step between academic research and problem solving in the public schools, and if the Kamehameha project demonstrated anything, it probably demonstrated the need for the creation of such entities. I'll just briefly sketch what happened. Twenty years ago Roland and I were given virtually unlimited authority and very ample funding to figure out why native Hawaiian children did not learn to read. The strategy was to assemble all the . . . knowledge that we had . . . and we were going to put all this knowledge together and assemble this group in this school we built, and we were going to solve this problem. Now some people would say that twenty years later we more or less did that. But it's often forgotten that for the first five years we were miserable failures. We had all these resources and all this knowledge. We had excellent teachers. We had everything going for us, but for five years we didn't do any better than the public schools. In the sixth year it started getting a little better. But it took ten years of university researchers of every stripe working every day with teachers. Ten years to figure out how to teach reading to first graders.

Now what's the message? The message is that the kinds of analyses that we hear about are terrific and I've learned a lot from this and from the journals. And I think the basic research must go on. We drew upon it and it was extremely valuable to us in the reading research. But I can also tell you that it is only the first little step for developing solutions to something like dropouts. What I fear is that it is not recognized that we simply don't have an institutional mechanism in the country by and large to have the activity setting that we were so lucky to have in Hawaii. I can assure you that this activity setting does not exist at UCLA. I haven't heard any evidence that at Stanford such an activity setting exists. There's no place in the country where this activity would exist in any way that is going to become sustained or work. You could find some isolated examples like the Kamehameha project . . . . Here's my hypothesis: until this becomes a routine part of all major funding projects, until this becomes a reality, there can be no change.

Nothing has changed since I was in first grade a long time ago. Teachers hand out ditto sheets and they do recitations. They make learning opportunities available and if students take advantage of it, fine. They give them feedback. But that's about it. And I'm not claiming our research is the basis of this . . . just look at the literature about it. I can't think of any major change in the public schools in the twenty years that I've been working. It's not going to go from academic discussion to change, because I think we're missing this intermediate institutional step. Oddly enough, most of us are outraged by the success with which hard sciences have been able to translate principles into weapons. But you'll notice that they way they do it is they don't rely strictly on university research. They have huge sustained research and development institutions that do it. In education we don't have that. And until we get wise that we have to have major long-term commitment of this sort we're not going to make any changes.

Robert Rueda: I'd like to concur with Ron and jump up the level of analysis a little higher. I'd also like to put on the table the proposition that we have sufficient theory and research right now to essentially alleviate the problem of dropouts. I don't see how putting more money into doing basic research on learning is the answer. I think we have sufficient information.

I'm reminded of an article that Ray (McDermott) did a long time ago, an example that really stuck with me that illustrates the problem. He did a microethnography of a low achieving kid in a reading group, working with a teacher from a different cultural background. At that point the cultural mismatch notion was a central explanation of why minorities don't do well in school. So if teachers and kids don't share the same cultural characteristics, it leads to serious problems and so forth. What he found was, it's sort of curious, that those kinds of things persist after months and months and years, and so on. How is it that kids that have basically intact cognitive capacities can't adjust to simple cultural conventions after a short period of time being together? McDermott's explanation was that when his turn to read came, the kid sort of turned away. He wasn't using the right conventions in order to get called on. The teacher also turned away. They colluded. It was just a way to avoid the problem. They were both doing something in conjunction as a way of dealing with this kid's poor achievement.

There are larger institutional factors than the simple cultural mismatch explanation. Look at the larger institutional setting. Do we really have a system right now that can handle the possibility of no dropouts? What if we did away with dropouts? Could the system really handle that? I really don't think that it could. What if all kids succeeded? What would happen to the kids?

I sat on an admissions committee at school. I've sat on personnel committees. There's a lot of screening that goes on. What if everyone could get a PhD? What if Stanford opened its doors? I really think it's something intrinsic to the system that we need failure. We made a conscious decision to need 25 per cent of the people as non-participants. There are larger economic questions. In my own field of special education there are whole industries and fields of specialization that are dependent on kids failing. What would school psychologists do if there were no tests to give? I wish I had stock in the WISC-R. I've been involved in a couple of court cases where I've had to review files. Every time a test is given, somebody's making money. So I think there are other things operating. I think we really have a solid (maybe not all the answers) body of theory and research. We may need a little bit more, but I think we can basically make a lot of headway with what we have. But there are these other factors that are intrinsic to the sysem at a structural level that we need to examine.

Concha Delgado-Gaitan: I think political economy has taught us that this country does need our reserve army of labor, so your questions are on target in terms of does this country need failure? I'd like to piggyback on some of the comments made on this question of change. I truly concur with the fact that we do have sufficient knowledge right now to solve the problems that we have. Certainly, though we can never stop learning, that is not the main point. The thing we don't know or maybe we're afraid to know is how long change really takes, what kind of commitment it takes to create the change that we've been talking about. With respect to the level of commitment that we have to that sustained continuation of research in one community to have an impact on some level, I think that it does require far more funding than we're ever allowed in education. But the other part of it is to what degree we utilize that base of knowledge we already have in a way that will impact at other levels such as policy.

To give a case in point of how some people are working with it, at the University of California, Santa Barbara is a group of researchers, part of the linguistic minority research project. One of the aims of this group is to look at the existing body of research and the continuing body of research generated in the linguistic minority communities and attempt to address some of the policy that the legislature is making here in California with respect to those issues. In late April there will be a conference in Santa Barbara where these researchers will be dialoging with policy-makers and attempting to influence them, and serve certainly not as lobbyists, but as real informants about what we do know works and doesn't work.

I also vacillate between frustration and elation. We know there is great value in the work we are doing, but because of the structure of the system we have little evidence that our sustained efforts have any impact on the system. However, were we not involved, we would continue to perpetuate those very recalcitrant kinds of behaviors that we have been criticizing. I would hope that we continue to use the knowledge that we have as a springboard to bring about and generate enthusiasm about impact at any level.

David Fetterman: This has been very interesting, listening to all the comments. All of us here are familiar with the fact that there has been a variety of programs and concerns about dropouts for years and years. It's like a pendulum. When a certain administration is in, different kinds of funding cycles are in. I still have a naive commitment to democratic ideals and believe that there should be a national agenda. But I saw what happened when a lot of the social welfare programs were decimated recently. A lot of friends working with social welfare programs or assessing them lost their jobs. There isn't, at this point, any clear leadership. It's interesting just to see the cycles go in and out, back and forth. It does make you a bit cynical at times, as to how far we're going to go with this cycle before we move on to the next phase of it again.

General Open Discussion

Larry Cuban, Moderator: We have heard from each member of the panel, so now it is time to have some responses and comments from the audience. I hope that you will feel free to react to the papers, the discussants' responses, the comments by panel members, or anything else that is germane to the purposes of this conference.

From the audience: I thought Valverde's was a remarkable dissenting viewpoint from many of the earlier talks, and intrinsic to his message is the fact that things are the way they are for no small purpose. It suits the referent society and the power structure to have things the way they are. We have to come to terms with the notion that institutional rigidity does not permit the addressing of this issue.

I see a lot of kids respond to the system by saying that the important thing they learned in school was that there are adults in positions of power who are lying and who are manipulating the system. To them that is more important than finishing school.

Another participant stated: I agree with your statements but I don't see how this is a dissenting view. It seems to me that this is exactly what was implicit in many papers and discussants' remarks, and explicit in some . . . that it suits the power structure to have about a 25 per cent dropout rate, for instance.

Pete Mesa, from the audience, stated that there is an absence of knowledge that gets from academics to practitioners. 'I don't think the university takes enough responsibility in organizing knowledge in such a way that it can be more useful to practitioners.'

Another audience member suggested: There needs to be a change in the economic and the business cycle, which would tend to make people look at what's going on a little more carefully, and then a change in the political climate. I would think . . . we should have more chance at the long-term funding we need, as suggested by Ron. I like the statement that someone made, 'We should use our anthropological right to claim our ignorance about what we see going on.' With that kind of understanding there may be more of a readiness to hear some of those things.

I also like the concept of a 'participation structure' and the fact that practitioners can make change in their own classrooms by changing the participation structure, and thus address the issue of alienation in a different way. So I'm glad to see the attention placed on this problem of dropouts because it lays the groundwork so when the policy-makers start to wake up, they have some place to turn to get some answers.

Reba Page (UC Riverside): We've heard a lot about variation in ethnic minorities, but we haven't heard very much about variations in the schools . . . . There are several studies that have been done about minority success even though they are in lower track classes in private and particularly Catholic schools, where the school culture does not define academic incompetence as necessarily exclusionary. It doesn't exclude you from the possibility of learning things in school and even from going on to college. Not even all magnet schools are the same. Magnet schools can define poor and minority children as able to learn and then can demonstrate higher academic achievement scores.... Our culture is not monolithic, we have traditions in which we have made some effort to be more than a mainstream white, Anglo, middle-class society. We have been a compassionate nation at some points in our history. Perhaps we need to retrieve those traditions in order to reconstitute the public faith about what public schools are for.

Another participant stated: When you have a WASP teacher working with students from a different cultural background, it's almost impossible to relate to that group because they have different world views. So you may need some very basic restructuring of the system. If you really want to understand the student you have ideally to experience the background from where that student comes from.

David Smith added that interested persons should add some sessions in Phoenix at the AAA conference to continue this discussion with anthropologists and people who have done research. Pete Mesa spoke again about not translating academic knowledge into a practical, useful focus on curriculum content and ideas. Training programs for teachers should add a component of how they should interact with children, with each other and with disabled students. One high school teacher from the audience wanted to bring the focus from the future to the present when she stated that she had to go back to school to face Tongan, Black and Hispanic students. She asked, 'What can I go back and tell my fellow teachers that we can do on Monday? I want "ACTION action". Where do you start?' A number of panelists attempt to answer the question.

Ray McDermott suggested looking at some of the programs currently working in East Harlem. He cited examples of a school district in which the students participate in community jobs.

There are a thousand things to do, none of which by themselves will work. It depends on how you try to understand them, depending on what you try to let them do . . . . I'm talking about a very different neighborhood. People in the community get involved. Meetings were held. All the kids succeeded very well.

The most important thing is they started to build the curriculum around experiences the kids were having. In other words, they turned the kids into ethnographers. The kids (aged 13–15, seventh and eighth graders) had to take notes. They were to write stories about what they were doing. Those were kids with very few chances, and they all went off to good high schools following that experience. It took a tremendous amount of energy and work. It all could have died on any given day . . . but I'm talking about the spirit of the thing. Namely they said from the beginning success was a possibility for every kid in the group. They threw no one out. The excitement of that work was the documentation of how many people tried to interfere with the project. The school board was a problem at one point. The teachers were upset with the work they had to do. Various people somewhere along the way tried to interfere for various reasons.

David Fetterman suggested 'career learning' as a viable alternative, a natural kind of motivation. The students would research jobs, invite speakers, work with people in various careers along the way. The program he worked with had as many counselors as teachers to work with the whole person, and their personal problems. He also suggested individualized instruction, so they could go at their own pace through various packets of material: '. . . the curriculum was sensitive to various cultures involved, in the program I was involved in. The programs were geared for Blacks, Hispanics and low-income Whites. The programs can be incorporated without a great deal of money but involving a great amount of hard work.'

One of the things educators want to do is *act* first, according to Leonard Valverde.

Let me caution you not to act but think first, gather information, rather than act. Effective school literature says get the principal to make this his or her priority; generate that commitment throughout the school; then teachers and administrators should get some people together who will examine the population, identify the forces driving these kids out and adversely affecting your population, so you have some data. Then when you have identified the forces pushing them out or affecting them adversely, then you start building some appropriate responses. Not all kids leave school for the same reasons, and you may have categories that you want to attend to that are context-specific to your population and resources. For example, if a school finds a large number of dropout pregnant teenagers after studying the population, then teachers and administrators should begin programs which would address this particular problem, as in developing a childcare system to bring the kids back. The problem is not so much global as it is specific to the population or situation itself.

He also said a problem exists in going from the theory to 'hands-on' solutions, for example, in the training of teachers.

Roland Tharp reiterated certain points as he addressed the question from the young teacher.

One should contextualize instruction, incorporate within instruction specific activities for language development. Conversation with each child should occur at least two times per week in small, culturally homogeneous groups. Try to attempt to observe the courtesies and conventions of the conversation. Motivational factors should be considered. In the social organization make sure there is a variety of instructional grouping including large groups, small groups, and dyads. Finally cognitive learning styles should represent a variety of structures.

A question was asked about what to do to individualize instruction culturally for each student when you have five or six culturally different groups in the classroom. David Fetterman suggested the key is to do what is contextually appropriate.

There is a definite danger, not just in stereotyping, but in undermining the students' own motivation. A number of individuals have mentioned today the necessity of being culturally and linguistically sensitive. When you are a little bit more sensitive to exactly who your students are, you can have an idea of what your group instructions need to be. Most people who have been teachers on any level know that. The key, I think, is to implement what is contextually appropriate, rather than follow rigidly a specific policy.

An audience member told about his experience: 'in a class I took at Stanford . . . I learned that the most important thing was to schedule a lot of activities where the students get a lot of exposure to each other and then they teach each other.'

Another audience participant suggested that researchers should put out their results to practitioners.

The point of researchers packaging their information so

practitioners can use it is very important . . . also, one of the things researchers might consider doing is when you go into schools, it might be interesting when studying students to work with the teachers, so that they see themselves as part of a team. When you include teachers in this way they not only feel part of the study, but it gives them an opportunity to learn and also to be advocates of the research, and users of the research.

David Smith mentioned the notion of cultural sensitivity.

One does not have to completely culturally understand the kids in order to respect them. I think if we start with the assumption that whatever a person is, is legitimate, that they're worthy of respect, that if in fact we live in that same world that they live in, we might act the same way they do, that it changes the way we look at them. It's not a matter of cultural sensitivity, it's a matter of recognizing that they are legitimate and worthy of respect. And don't make the goal one of understanding and then respond on the basis of that understanding, but make the goal to respect them and recognize that we don't understand and we can't understand.

One member of the audience commented that there were no black people on the panel. Henry Trueba mentioned that Professor John Ogbu was invited, but could not attend. It was suggested that a special effort be made in the future to insure the panel was well-rounded and included black members.

Perry Gilmore noted that rank is pervasive in the school setting, as much as it is on the African Savannah.

One of the nicest things I have learned about being human is that you didn't have to accept rank . . . but we will probably still have tracking. One of the things that is constant that I've seen as an educator and a primary school teacher, employed in teacher vocabularies, curriculum development vocabularies, and cited in linguistic vocabularies, as well as larger socio-cultural micro- and macro-vocabularies is *tracking*. We ignore it. It's ingrained in our system and Kenneth Goodman said it best when he said that 'Special Education is America's answer to desegregation'. If we don't look at tracks, at what they're doing, I think we are being absolutely criminal in avoiding the actual one mechanism that we have that assures dropouts, illiteracy, and school failure.

Concluding Remarks

In his concluding remarks Henry Trueba said:

> The issue of the distance between practitioners and teachers and researchers needs to be a central issue especially in studying the organization of structures that allow you to team up with people. The second thing that has to be discussed at length and that goes beyond the school and teachers is the family and the role of women in knowledge acquisition of children. The family and the role of the family is the natural unit where 'first knowledge' is organized. Finally, as researchers we are 'snobs' in the overspecialization of knowledge. We have become snobs in the way we overspecialize ourselves in our research. Sometimes we ignore the knowledge accumulated by people who have come before us and the people who are doing practical work on the problem. The power and continuity of that knowledge is something we cannot take as trivial.'

In his concluding remarks, George Spindler said:

> As I look back upon what has happened today I am pleased about what we have done. It is true that we have addressed what to do on Monday morning only indirectly, for the most part. Practical applications of what we know must be developed. Translations of the native language of the academy into the vernacular of everyday problem solving are essential. But we have done more of this than we give ourselves credit for: the papers by Trueba, Tharp, Gilmore and Smith, are very close to being programmatic recommendations. Comments by each of the discussants in one way or another showed their concern with the application of our accumulated understandings to the amelioration of conditions in schools that lead to dropping out. There is the realization, however, that schools can only do so much. Schools exist within, and depend upon larger social, cultural, economic and political environments that influence, often determine, whether children stay in school or drop out. This should not lead us to a hopeless or fatalistic attitude, but to a realism that can help guide us to workable programs of change.
> What we have done with great success in this conference, I believe, is to show that dropping out, or conversely, staying in, is not a singular process to be understood in isolation. It is a process imbedded in every other aspect of school life and the

life of the community, in both the broader and narrower sense, that the school serves.

We observe that the majority of mainstream students do not drop out. Our attempts to understand why they do not are crucial to understanding why some mainstream and many minority students *do* dropout. A substantial number of minority students stay in school despite great obstacles to staying in, and we have analyzed many of those obstacles today. Understanding why they stay in is a major step toward finding out why some drop out. And the finding that certain immigrant minorities with what seem to be barriers of cultural differences and language greater than those facing indigenous minorities, drop out less often and stay in school longer, gives us further insight into staying in (and dropping out).

It seems that we need failure if we have success, in our competitive, individualistic society, and that we have constructed a multi-billion dollar industry of testing, sorting, and predicting success and failure, and the degrees in between. Our culturally patterned preoccupation with success and failure is a part of the problem.

Our final question then becomes one that is a hidden agenda in much of the conference and explicit here and there ... why do young people stay in school? What motivates them to endure imprisonment (in Valverde's terms), to endure busy work (in Rueda's), to survive the horrendous conditions of the inner city and the ghetto school (in Suarez-Orozco's analysis)? The answer seems to lie in the direction that Louise and I tried to enunciate in our paper, and that Ray McDermott carried further — that they believe that they will become 'Hutterites' ... they will succeed and be accepted. They will have access to the privileges of the mainstream in American life. The thread of motivation is apparently broken for many minority youth, who don't see or believe in the connection, or having seen it don't think the gain is worth the pain.

Our problem may be less the dropouts than the stay-ins. If we understand the latter we will understand the former. Perhaps then we can take 'action action', in the words of one of our participants from the floor.

In conclusion to my remarks and this conference, let me say that I always stand in awe, whenever I do anything of this kind or come to an affair of this sort, at the enormous knowledge of my colleagues and their tremendous talent. I always feel very humble. But today I feel humble in another way, too. And that is I am most appreciative of the questions and comments from the participating audience. I'm awfully glad that you came. So that's all, and thank you very much for coming and participating.

Index